CAPE WINELANDS

A Touring Guide to Wineries of
Constantia, Stellenbosch, Franschhoek & Paarl

CAPE WINELANDS

A Touring Guide to Wineries of
Constantia, Stellenbosch, Franschhoek & Paarl

THERESA MORRISON

PHOTOGRAPHY BY LANZ VON HÖRSTEN

David Philip
Cape Town

Published by David Philip Publishers (Pty) Ltd,
208 Werdmuller Centre, Newry Street, Claremont 7708, Cape Town, South Africa

ISBN 0-86486-459-0

Text © 2000 by Theresa Morrison
Photographs © 2000 by Lanz von Hörsten
Design by Sarah-Anne Raynham
Maps by Ernst-Reiner Klaus

Reproduction by Virtual Colour, Cape Town
Printed by Creda Press, Cape Town

CONTENTS

AUTHOR'S NOTE

In researching this book, I did not seek or accept any gifts. I visited each winery as an ordinary visitor, took standard tours where available and wandered about the wineries. At no time during my research and writing did I advise the wineries of my activities nor did I give them any indication of my intent.

The views expressed in this book are my own and do not necessarily reflect the views of others. There are many wineries in the Cape that produce excellent wine and offer pleasant experiences. It was not practicable to include every one of them in this guide. There are a number of publications that provide comprehensive overviews of all the wineries and their wine. I have listed the more popular books at the back of this guide.

To all the wineries in the Cape, thank you for making this beautiful part of the world so special.

Please send your views, experiences, suggestions and comments to me,
Theresa Morrison, at:
PO Box 51303
Waterfront 8002
Cape Town, South Africa
Tel/Fax: +27 21 790 4586
Or e-mail to : wine@34south.com
www.34south.com
I'd love to hear from you.

To Kim with joy: your artistic insight and imagination are a constant inspiration

WELCOME TO THE CAPE WINELANDS

The wine farms at the foot of Africa nestle beneath dramatic mountains. Their history is long and fascinating; the culture eclectic; the architecture unique; the scenery breathtaking. And the wine: the wines are legendary.

The winelands of the Cape are beautiful and overwhelming, both for their setting and for the sheer number of estates. This guide has been conceived in response to the questions I am often asked: 'Where do we go? Which estates should we visit?' These are daunting questions to answer, not least because it is so difficult to know the experience each person is seeking. Is it the wine? What type? What style? Is it the atmosphere of the winery? Or the tour? Or the family touch? The flamboyant winemaker? The technical winemaker? The vast cellars? The intimate cellars? The architecture? The gardens? The food? The breathtaking views? The combinations are endless but the goal is common: to have a pleasant and memorable day.

With well over 300 wineries, it is vital to have a foretaste of what you want to experience – or you could find yourself spending most of the day in the car! Unlike Napa Valley and most regions in France, the Cape winelands cover a vast expanse of the Western Cape. Technically, there are twelve districts spread over hundreds of kilometres. Fortunately from a touring perspective, there are five areas close to Cape Town where much of the estate wine is grown and produced. These are Constantia, Durbanville, Paarl, Franschhoek and Stellenbosch. Because of their proximity to each other as well as to Cape Town, it is

possible to enjoy a pleasant drive touring several of the areas in one day. Those interested in venturing further afield for a few days should refer to some of the books listed towards the back of this guide.

The wines of the Cape have been heaped with rave reviews and it is difficult to go wrong on a touring day. But there is more to the winelands than wine alone. In the Cape, there are magnificent examples of architecture in truly sensational mountain settings, creating an atmosphere not to be found in any other wine region of the world. Unlike other wine guides, *Cape Winelands* features winery tours organised by region, architecture, cultural interests, season, technical orientation and other special interests. The estates selected in this guide are known for their wonderful wines. Each is visitor-friendly. Each has also a special character to make your day enjoyable.

Cape Winelands is not a technical treatise on winemaking or a professional critique on wine quality. Nor is it an exhaustive review of all the wineries in the Cape. It gives you a glimpse of wineries and their regions, animated by their colourful histories and warmed by their individual stories. The wineries featured in this guide are those which I have recommended to friends and family over the years depending upon their specific points of interest. My list is limited so as not to be overwhelming for the day-tripper. There is much more to the winelands of the Cape, and by all means explore them as much as you can. They are special places that bloom with beauty every time you visit them.

TOURING, TASTING, AND USING THIS GUIDE

USING THIS GUIDE

Cape Winelands assists you in visualising the experience offered by the wineries selected in this book. The objective is to help you decide where to focus your limited time so as to make the most of your day. It is designed primarily for day trips and short stays. Because of the number of wineries and the numerous possible combinations of excursions, *Cape Winelands* identifies the characteristics most sought by visitors touring the Cape winelands. These have been annotated in the next section. A winery singled out for, say, the Cape Dutch architecture will be notable for this specific feature. Other wineries might also have a similar characteristic but have not been identified as such because it is not as prominent. Again, this was done to simplify the seemingly endless choices faced by visitors. Mix and match according to your own interests.

There is a map on the inside front cover that gives a bird's-eye view of where the wineries are in relation to each other and to Cape Town. These wineries have provided much pleasure for myself, my family and friends. Create your own combinations. Enjoy your day and your stay.

EXPLANATORY NOTE:
In terms of trade agreements, common names for certain wines and spirits have had to be changed.

Cap classique is a sparkling wine fermented using the traditional methods employed in the Champagne district.

Port and sherry are to be renamed soon.

TOURING FACTS

Most regions have wine route associations which comprise member wineries. It is not compulsory to be a member of an association. Some wineries in this guide are members – others are not.

Other than Vergelegen, the wineries in this guide do not charge an entrance fee. Some may charge tour fees and/or a nominal amount for tasting, usually because of the high rate of glass breakage. Smoking is not allowed on tours, in cellars or in the tasting rooms. It is illegal to serve wine to anyone under 18 years of age. Check the individual winery details for opening times, cellar tours and seasonal issues.

For cellar and operations tours, be considerate and arrive at least five minutes before the scheduled tour. Several wineries will take you around if you book in advance, even if they do not offer regularly scheduled tours.

Wineries are cool, so take a jersey or light jacket. There can be a dramatic difference between the outside temperature and that of the tasting room, especially in the operational areas and the cellars, where wines are stored at ±15°C (59°F). It is best to wear closed-toed, rubber-soled shoes. Wineries maintain a high standard of cleanliness – it is crucial in their business. As a result, the floors are rinsed often and can be slippery. Remember, wineries are farms. It is most likely that you will walk across areas that have not been paved. The ground may be loose, dusty or muddy.

The owners, winemakers and staff at the wineries love what they do and are proud of their wines and wineries. Don't be shy to ask questions and take photographs.

TASTING

Whether you are a novice or a seasoned wine critic, enjoying wine is a personal experience. There is likely to be a wide variety of knowledge and depth of senses amongst the people in any tasting room. Do not be inhibited by the wine-speak. If you are interested in describing the smell, feel and taste, an aroma wheel will help you to find the words. These are not definitive terms. Use any word that you think describes what you smell or taste. Most importantly, simply enjoy the wine.

The water jugs on the tasting counters are there to rinse your glass between wines as well as for drinking. There are buckets on the tasting counters in which to discard the wine in your glass or the wine in your mouth. You may feel awkward at first but it is socially acceptable to 'spit' and even expected in the wine industry.

Please avoid drinking and driving on a wine tour. Dedicate a driver at the outset. To ensure that everyone has an opportunity to enjoy the wines on offer, we usually alternate the driver on different days.

PHYSICALLY DISABLED VISITORS

Most wineries have facilities to enable wheelchair access to the tasting rooms. Many are easily accessible. Some are more difficult. A few winery tours are accessible to people in wheelchairs but it is advisable to discuss this with the winery when you book the tour. Tour guides who offer professional assistance are listed in the reference section at the end of the book.

SEASONS

All of the wineries are wonderful to visit throughout the year. Cape weather can be fickle, with winter weather in summer and summer weather in winter. It is advisable to layer yourself with jerseys or sweaters throughout the year.

WINERIES RECOMMENDED FOR YOUR SPECIAL INTERESTS

CONSTANTIA

Cape Dutch homes:	Groot Constantia, Steenberg
Historical interest:	Groot Constantia, Klein Constantia
Gardens:	Groot Constantia, Buitenverwachting, Steenberg
Warm winter hearth:	Steenberg
Exquisite vistas:	Groot Constantia, Steenberg
Picnic ambience:	Groot Constantia
Winery restaurants:	Buitenverwachting, Groot Constantia, Steenberg
Other restaurants:	La Colombe, River Café, Uitsig
Interesting for kids:	Groot Constantia
Cap classique:	Buitenverwachting, Klein Constantia
Port:	Groot Constantia
Noble late harvest:	Klein Constantia
Tours:	Groot Constantia, Klein Constantia
Talking wine:	Klein Constantia

STELLENBOSCH

Cape Dutch homes:	Hazendal, Lievland, Meerlust, Rustenberg, Vergelegen, Vriesenhof, Zevenwacht
Historical interest:	Meerlust, Muratie, Rustenberg
Gardens:	Neil Ellis, Vergelegen
Warm winter hearth:	Hartenberg, Hazendal, Lievland, Rustenberg, Thelema, Vriesenhof
Exquisite vistas:	Amani, Camberley, Laibach, Longridge, Muratie, Neil Ellis, Thelema, Verdun, Vriesenhof
Picnic ambience:	Amani, Muratie, Verdun, Zevenwacht
Winery restaurants:	Blaauwklippen, Hartenberg, Hazendal, Morgenhof, Zevenwacht
Other restaurants:	96 Winery Road, Spier, La Masseria
Interesting for kids:	Blaauwklippen, Vergelegen, Zevenwacht
Cultural, art & other:	Amani, Hazendal, Muratie, Spier
Cap classique:	Longridge, Morgenhof
Port:	Morgenhof, Muratie, Rustenberg
Noble late harvest:	Lievland, Morgenhof, Vergelegen
Pinotage:	Kanonkop, Laibach, Longridge, Morgenhof, Neil Ellis, Vriesenhof, Warwick, Zevenwacht
Cellars:	Morgenhof, Vergelegen
Talking wine:	Camberley, Meerlust, Stonewall, Thelema, Vriesenhof

FRANSCHHOEK

Cape Dutch homes:	Boschendal, Mont Rochelle
Historical interest:	Boschendal
Gardens:	Boschendal
Warm winter hearth:	Haute Cabrière
Exquisite vistas:	Boekenhoutskloof, Dieu Donné, Mont Rochelle
Picnic ambience:	Boschendal, Dieu Donné, Mont Rochelle
Winery restaurants:	Boschendal, Haute Cabrière, Môreson
Other restaurants:	La Petite Ferme, Le Quartier Français
Interesting for kids:	Boschendal
Cap classique:	Boschendal, Cabrière, Dieu Donné
Noble late harvest:	Boschendal, Dieu Donné
Pinotage:	Dieu Donné, Môreson
Cellars:	Haute Cabrière
Tours:	Boschendal, Cabrière
Self-guided tours:	Boschendal
Talking wine:	Boekenhoutskloof

PAARL–DURBANVILLE

Gardens:	Backsberg
Exquisite vistas:	Glen Carlou, Rhebokskloof
Picnic ambience:	Backsberg
Winery restaurants:	Rhebokskloof
Other restaurants:	Bosman's
Interesting for kids:	Backsberg, Rhebokskloof
Cap classique:	Backsberg, Villiera
Brandy:	Backsberg
Port:	Glen Carlou, Villiera
Pinotage:	Backsberg, Nitida, Rhebokskloof, Villiera
Cellars:	Backsberg
Self-guided tours:	Backsberg, Villiera
Talking wine:	Nitida, Veenwouden, Villiera, Welgemeend

Constantia

Like all the wine areas in the Cape, the Constantia Valley is steeped in history. This valley is the queen mother of the Cape's wine-producing areas. When the Dutch East India Company established a refreshment station at the Cape, they sent Jan van Riebeeck as Commander. Trained as a physician, he quickly noticed significantly fewer incidences of scurvy on ships where wine was the staple drink. He appealed to his superiors in Holland to allow him to plant vines as part of the farming activities in the Cape. Despite concerns about drunken sailors, the Heren XVII granted Van Riebeeck's plea and vineyards were planted in the Company Gardens in the centre of Cape Town in 1655. The Houses of Parliament would later be built overlooking these gardens.

Although the winemaking was rudimentary, Van Riebeeck successfully produced wine some four years later in 1659. After an unsuccessful attempt in Green Point, farmers began to establish vineyards at the foot of Devil's Peak along the banks of the Liesbeek River. In their ignorance, the fields were planted too closely and could not be tended with animal-drawn ploughs. As a result of this as well as the growing needs of agriculture, some 200 slaves from Madagascar and Malaysia were brought to the Cape. The complex fabric of South Africa was thus partly woven by the introduction of these vines.

It was the later Commander and Governor, Simon van der Stel, who placed the Cape on the wine map. During his tenure (1679–99), Van der Stel was probably tolerated rather than liked. But he did have the vision and wherewithal to establish the Cape settlement as a self-sufficient colony. Van der Stel owned vineyards in Holland and, upon his arrival at the Cape, introduced new methods of planting, harvesting and vinification, including barrel cleanliness and fining. He also introduced the concept of crop balance to temper the fickleness of nature on the farmers' fortunes and to ensure the permanence of the Cape Colony. To demonstrate his teachings, Van der Stel astutely arranged to have a land grant of 770 hectares awarded to himself. This he called Constantia. He succeeded in producing a fortified, sweet wine that was favoured in Holland and England. Van der Stel built a modest homestead, where he retired and tended his vineyards until his death in 1712. The original Constantia estate was portioned into three properties shortly after Van der Stel's death: Bergvliet, De Hoop op Constantia and Constantia.

It was another sixty years before there was another passionate and acclaimed owner of Constantia – the Hendrik Cloete family. The Cloetes' most renowned wine, Vin de Constance, became the toast of European leaders, society and royalty. In particular, it was

favoured by Napoleon while exiled on St Helena. It also graced the tables of Bismarck and King Louis-Philippe of France, and was exalted in the writings of Jane Austen, Dickens and Baudelaire.

There remain four estates from the original Constantia – Groot Constantia, Klein Constantia, Buitenverwachting and Constantia Uitsig. Steenberg was established in 1682, when the southern part of Constantia Valley was awarded to Catharina Ustings Ras. Each of these estates has an illustrious history spanning the 350 years of winemaking at the Cape.

Vin de Constance? The recipe was lost over the years but the winemakers at Klein Constantia have now meticulously – and with a bit of good fortune – re-created this gold-in-a-glass, awarding-winning dessert wine.

The name Buitenverwachting means 'beyond expectations'. Nestling on the slopes of the Constantiaberg, the estate boasts wine and culinary feats that go indeed beyond one's expectations. So too does the viticulture. At Buitenverwachting, the gospel is harmonious farming. Ducks to gobble the dreaded snails and a herd of cows to provide natural fertiliser are just a few of the earth-friendly policies that have been implemented successfully.

Entering the bucolic estate, the driveway wanders under oaks nearly as old as Buitenverwachting. Rounding a bend, the manor house strikes a magnificent pose across the vineyard. Horses amble in the paddocks and guinea fowl scatter across the drive. It takes almost a full circle to meander to the tasting centre. At the last turn, the drive opens onto a parkland square. The classic U-shape of the homestead is distinctly visible in the distance. The simple 'home' on the north was the original cellar, opposite the slave quarters. The old barn, now converted to offices, completes the quadrangle. All these buildings reveal an elegant, historic architecture.

The tasting centre, by contrast, consists of sheets of glass, strips of wood and scores of linear geometry. Housed in the glass cavalcade between the offices and the restaurant, the tasting room is an exercise in the rational architecture of functional modernism.

When the Mueller family bought Buitenverwachting in the 1980s, it was derelict and threatened with urban development. Not only did they restore the estate's heritage but also established its pre-eminence in the modern wine world. The history of Buitenverwachting dates to 1773, when it was established as a separate property of 200 morgen from the Bergvliet Estate. Arend Brink soon acquired the land and built the manor house, Buitenverwachting, thereby giving the estate its name. (He also owned and named Schoongezicht near Stellenbosch.) It was not long before Brink sold to the Cloete family at Groot Constantia. In 1825, the Cloetes planted some 90 000 vines and, primarily due to this effort, Buitenverwachting has maintained its position as a wine farm.

Klein Constantia Road
Tel: (021) 794-5190/1
e-mail: buiten@pixie.co.za

WINEMAKER: Hermann Kirschbaum
OWNER: The Muellers
MANAGER: Lars Maack

OPEN: 9–5 Mon to Fri; 9–1 Sat
CLOSED: Public holidays

TOURS: None
TASTINGS: Nominal charge. Not deductible from price of wine purchased
WINES OFFERED FOR TASTING: Blanc blend, Sauvignon Blanc, Chardonnay, Rhine Riesling, Cabernet Sauvignon, Merlot, Brut Cap Classique

RESTAURANT: 794-3522 Reservations required; Elegant dress code Lunch/dinner: Tue–Fri; Dinner only: Sat
PICNICS: Not accommodated

The grande dame of the valley, Groot Constantia is rich in historical and cultural significance. The country road leads you through vineyards under cover of oaks. To catch sight of the gates is enough to sense the boundless ideals that created her.

Through Simon van der Stel's leading efforts, winemaking became a viable activity at the Cape. He established a model winery and developed the mountain slopes into vineyards. He named his new home 'Constantia', where he built a modest homestead known now as Groot Constantia.

The Constantia portion of Van der Stel's original estate was bought by Hendrik Cloete in 1773, and it was Cloete who put Constantia wines on the tables of the world. He also renovated the homestead, turning it into a stately manor house. It was a period of prosperity. Through bequest and inheritance, the property was divided into Groot and Klein Constantia. Groot Constantia was eventually sold to the Cape colonial government in 1885 when lean years took their toll on the Cloete heirs. In 1993 the South African government restored the neglected estate to its historic beauty.

The magnificence of the manor house combines strength and elegance. The simplicity of architectural lines and classical symmetry are complemented by the careful positioning of ornamental detail. Neither overpowers the other. They simply blend in sonorous harmony. The *jonkershuis* flanks the manor house and presently is home to a cozy restaurant. The building was originally a 'young man's house', typically built for the eldest son of the estate. The architecture is modest, befitting the junior standing of its intended inhabitants.

There are many aspects of Groot Constantia to explore. Compare the different styles of original wagons in the stables behind the *jonkershuis*. Review the history of the estate and the 1993 renovations. Explore the extensive wine museum, with its fascinating artefacts and utensils from ancient Greece to the nineteenth century. Don't miss the exquisite sculpture by Anton Anreith on the gable of the Cloete cellar behind the manor house. It ranks as one of the architect's finest artistic creations.

Stroll down the pedestrian mall to the manor house or wander to the Triton pool amongst the vineyards. Groot Constantia is a magic setting for picnics on its shaded lawns overlooking False Bay and the surrounding mountains.

Groot Constantia Road
Tel: (021) 794-5128
e-mail: gct@mweb.co.za

WINEMAKER: Bob de Villiers
OWNER: Groot Constantia Trust
MANAGER: Danie Appel

OPEN: 10–5 every day; 9–6 in summer
CLOSED: Christmas, New Year's Day, Good Friday

TOURS: On the hour 10–4.
Booking essential. Nominal cost
TASTINGS: Nominal charge for 5 wines.
Not deductible from price of wine purchased
WINES OFFERED FOR TASTING:
Sauvignon Blanc, Chardonnay, Weisser Riesling, Cabernet Sauvignon, Shiraz, Red blends, Port

SHOP: Souvenirs
RESTAURANT: Tavern 794-1144: daily 10–6; Fri & Sat 10am–11pm
Jonkershuis 794-6255: daily 9am–late
PICNICS: Order through Jonkershuis

KLEIN CONSTANTIA

Klein Constantia Road
Tel: (021) 794-5188
e-mail: kleincon@global.co.za
www.kleinconstantia.com

WINEMAKER: Ross Gower
OWNER: Duggie & Lowell Jooste

OPEN: 9–5 Mon to Fri ; 9–1 Sat
CLOSED: Christmas, Good Friday

TOURS: By appointment
TASTINGS: No charge for individuals
WINES OFFERED FOR TASTING:
    Sauvignon Blanc, Sémillon,
    Chardonnay, Rhine Riesling, Cabernet
    Sauvignon, Shiraz, Red blend

SHOP: Souvenirs
RESTAURANT: None
PICNICS: Not accommodated

The road leading to both Klein Constantia and Buitenverwachting winds through rural Constantia. The homestead hides in the oaks and the few glimpses of its façade reveal an exquisite example of early Cape Dutch architecture. Admire it as you first enter the estate – it's the best view of the manor house you'll get. In the parking area take note of the old cork trees providing shade.

The Klein Constantia winery has a friendly architecture. There are windows over-looking the fermentation tanks and the bottling line. The maturation barrels fill the arch-ways below. In the wide and expansive tasting area you will be treated to luscious wines by friendly, well-informed guides. Although their most famous wine may be the Vin de Constance, don't overlook the others, many of which have been bedecked with numerous awards over the past twenty years. If you have the time, book a winery tour for a personal and down-to-earth peek at the awards-in-waiting.

As with all the Constantia estates, Klein Constantia has a long and revered history. It is now home to Vin de Constance, a re-creation of the famed sweet wine that was the toast of the rich and famous in Europe some 200 years ago. When the Joostes acquired Klein Constantia in 1980, they began a quest to re-create Hendrik Cloete's Vin de Constance. Through their research, they were able to craft a wine that they believed was very close to the original – and found they were right when the Duke of Northumberland discovered a bottle of the original in the vast underground cellar at his family estate. Only made when the conditions are right, it is bottled in a similar fashion to the original. And it is special.

Another famous owner of Klein Constantia was Sir Abraham Lochner de Villiers and his wealthy wife, Clara Hussey. An American heiress to a Pittsburgh steel fortune, she introduced glamour and gaiety. In the early twentieth century, they beguiled Capetonians and dignitaries with swank parties. Klein Constantia's most exotic 'guest', however, was Sheikh Abdurahman Matebe Shah. One of the last sultans of Malacca, he was captured by the Dutch in Sumatra and banished to the wild bush of Constantia. In addition to being the leader of a nation, the Sheikh was a spiritual leader, important in introducing Islam to South Africa. The *kramat* at the entrance of Klein Constantia was built on the spot where he was thought to have died in 1681 or 1682. It forms part of the 'Holy Circle' which con-sists of several important Islamic burial tombs, or *kramats*, around the Peninsula.

The winery at Steenberg shares the vast estate with a quiet hotel, a first-class golf course and an exclusive residential community. There are two entrances to Steenberg. Access to the winery is through the south gate, past the famous Pollsmoor Prison. After the imposing security entrance, turn first left. Because the entrance is different from that of most wineries, it can be confusing initially, but persevere as the short wait while signing in is worth every moment.

The winery is a new building set high on the mountainside, surrounded by vineyards. Created in a Cape vernacular style, overlooking the Constantiaberg, it has generous proportions reflecting the estate's historical identity. Only the sliding doors hint at the avant-garde heart of this winery: a hi-tech, cutting-edge cellar.

The wine guides are attentive and well versed. Relax and explore their wines in your own way. The guides are happy to assist as much – or as little – as you want.

One of the first land grants issued by Simon van der Stel, the estate dates back to 1682. Its first owner, Catharina Ustings Ras, managed to convince Van der Stel to sell her the land – highly irregular, as women were not allowed to buy land and only in certain circumstances could they inherit it.

The original homestead is gone: most likely it was replaced by the second owner of Steenberg, who bought the property in 1695. This surviving homestead has been meticulously restored, and is graced by a classical rose and herb garden. It takes but a short, extra drive to the restaurant area to see these magnificent buildings and wander through the quiet *werf* garden.

The focal point is the restaurant housed in the original wine cellar. Historically and architecturally interesting, its interior has been refurbished in a traditional style. The menu is Continental with a dash of traditional South African fare. During the day, sit under the oaks and absorb the serene beauty of the Constantia Valley.

Steenberg Road
Tel: (021) 713-2211
e-mail: info@steenbrg.co.za

WINEMAKER: Nicky Versfeld
OWNER: Johnnies Industrial Corp
MANAGER: Herman Hanekom

OPEN: 8:30–4:30 Mon to Fri;
9–1 Sat in Sept to Feb
CLOSED: Public holidays

TOURS: By appointment
TASTINGS: Nominal charge
WINES OFFERED FOR TASTING:
Sauvignon Blanc, Sémillon,
Chardonnay, Cabernet Sauvignon,
Merlot

RESTAURANT: Breakfast 7–10;
Lunch 12–2:30; Dinner 7–10:30
PICNICS: Not accommodated

Stellenbosch

The 'mountains of Africa' surrounding Stellenbosch are dramatic and seemingly impenetrable. Their bluish, purple faces change character throughout the day as the sunlight transforms their chiselled peaks. Ranges like Helderberg, Jonkershoek, Simonsberg and Drakenstein each have their unique character – sometimes sharp and jagged, sometimes buckled and gnarled, and at yet other times bold and strong.

It was to this boundary of Africa that Simon van der Stel ventured in search of fertile land. He imagined a town surrounded by vineyards and agricultural activities. And thus Stellenbosch was born. It was an important establishment in the history of the Cape for, until this time, the Dutch East India Company had to import food to sustain its base at the foot of Africa. As Eastern goods became more and more fashionable during the 17th century, so trade between East and West expanded. This may have secured the importance of the fledgeling Cape Town but it also increased its population and the demand for fresh provisions. Thanks in parts to the settlement at the foot of the Hottentots-Holland Mountains, the Cape became self-sufficient.

Stellenbosch was established in 1680 when eight families settled on the new land on the banks of the Eerste River. By 1685, most of the presently well-known farms had been granted. It did not take long before many of the Stellenbosch farms became linked together in some way through marriage, inheritance, insolvency or intrigue. The stories are fascinating and colourful. Most of the wineries have chronicled their history. Often, they have remarkable tales to share or books to offer.

Stellenbosch retains its village atmosphere with a rural sophistication. It is cosmopoli-

STELLENBOSCH WINERIES BY ROUTE

BOTTELARY RD (M23)	R44 NORTH	POLKADRAAI RD (M12)	R44 SOUTH
Hartenberg	Kanonkop	Amani	Blaauwklippen
Hazendal	Laibach	Verdun	Longridge
Zevenwacht	Lievland	Zevenwacht	Stonewall
	Morgenhof		Vriesenhof
	Muratie		
	Warwick		

tan in many ways, being home to outdoor concerts, art exhibitions, drama productions and people who appreciate and enjoy the subtle charms of life. It is also a vibrant university town. Strings of art galleries, antique stores, coffee shops and interesting restaurants line its historic and beautiful streets. Church Street and Dorp Street are full of restored buildings from various architectural eras. Andringa Street is a must for those who enjoy shops and galleries.

Stellenbosch is also the heart of South Africa's wine industry. From the undulating hills to the deep glens of the mountain ranges, the land is planted with vines. Excellent wineries abound, and I often find it difficult to decide which direction to take. To help minimise this dilemma, I have marked Stellenbosch into several main routes: Bottelary Rd (M23), Polkadraai Rd (M12), R44 South (from Stellenbosch to Somerset West), R44 North (from Stellenbosch to Paarl) and the Helshoogte Pass (R310 from Stellenbosch to Franschhoek). The Jonkershoek Valley is a destination on its own. Meerlust is situated on the R310 leading from the N2 towards Stellenbosch.

JONKERSHOEK
Neil Ellis

HELSHOOGTE PASS (R310)
Camberley
Rustenberg
Thelema

R310 FROM THE N2
Meerlust

SOMERSET WEST
Vergelegen

And now, as they say, for something completely different: a modern, Afro-European winery. The stunning selection of African art and artefacts on sale is worth the trip to this special, boutique winery – not to mention the attractive wines. The bottles sport little works of art as well, with an unusual motif that you can keep: a whimsical memento.

'Amani' is a Swahili word meaning 'peace' – a witticism of the owners, the Makepeaces. Mark Makepeace's enthusiasm and abundant optimism are as infectious as his smile. An ex-advertising man, he has a swift eye for aesthetics and a keen understanding of what consumers are looking for. At Amani, both Mark and his wife Hillary add a fresh sense to what it means to go to the winelands.

The buildings are elegant industrial chic. The tasting area is light and airy with double-volume glass windows and beechwood and metal fittings. The permanent display of art lends a balanced note to the clean lines. The art for sale is displayed around the tasting room, adding to the interest of this unique winery. Upstairs is a veranda overlooking the verdant valleys of Stellenbosch against the backdrop of the mountains. It's a great place to take your own picnic.

Amani introduced its maiden vintage in 1997 and took home Veritas awards for all of its wines. While Amani is a new winery and the Makepeaces new to winemaking, they are not new to the wine industry. The family is connected with the venerable Klein Constantia Estate, which has provided technical support and a lot of enthusiasm – if it's possible to add any more enthusiasm to the effervescent team at this winery.

If Mark Makepeace is around, a tour is a must. He delights in the winery and is a spontaneous and interesting guide, sharing unusual facts and insights. The tour feels more like a friend showing you around his new house.

Polkadraai Road (M12)
Tel: (021) 905-1126
e-mail: wine@amani.co.za

WINEMAKER: Mark Makepeace
OWNER: Mark and Hillary Makepeace

OPEN: Oct–Mar 10–4 Mon–Sun;
   Apr–Sept 10–4 Tue–Fri, 10–1:30 Sat
CLOSED: Public Holidays

TOURS: By appointment
TASTINGS: No charge for individuals
WINES OFFERED FOR TASTING:
   Sauvignon Blanc, Chardonnay, Chenin
   Blanc, Noble Late Harvest, Merlot

SHOP: Art and souvenirs
RESTAURANT: None
PICNICS: Bring your own

BLAAUWKLIPPEN

R44 South
(Stellenbosch–Somerset West)
Tel: (021) 880-0133
e-mail: mail@blaauwklippen.com
www.blaauwklippen.com

WINEMAKER: Hein Hesebeck
OWNER: Blaauwklippen Agricultural
    Estate (Pty) Ltd

OPEN: 9–5 Mon–Fri; 9–1 Sat
CLOSED: 25 & 26 December, New Year's
    Day, Good Friday

TOURS: 11 and 3 Mon–Fri
TASTINGS: Moderate charge
WINES OFFERED FOR TASTING: Chenin
    Blanc, Sauvignon Blanc, Chardonnay,
    Chardonnay–Sémillon, Cabernet
    Sauvignon, Merlot, Pinotage, Shiraz,
    Zinfandel, Late Harvest, Port

SHOP: Souvenirs
RESTAURANT: Pub lunch 12–3 Mon–Sat
PICNICS: Not accommodated

FESTIVALS & PROGRAMMES: Horse-
    drawn carriage rides, museum,
    leather workshop

If Blaauwklippen weren't a wine farm, it would be a saloon in the Wild West. Rustic and charming, the tasting room is long and spacious with a separate room at the end full of old yellowwood tables and riempie chairs. Whether you stand around 'shooting the hay' at the tasting bar or 'try your hand' at a table, Blaauwklippen oozes a snug naturalness.

In the very back there is a museum display of antique furniture including an enormous ornate organ, various chests and all manner of household items and farming tools. They have recently added some historic brandy pots to the collection. In the shed outside behind the pony corral, there are dozens of old carriages and vintage cars on display. It's an enthusiast's delight.

In the summer, mosey through the vineyards in a horse-drawn carriage. As you sip your wine, settle into the romantic clippity-clop ambling of the horses. The carriage ride is also a great diversion for children, who may ride unaccompanied while you enjoy the wine tasting. With no set timetable for the trip, it easily fits into your day.

At the leather studio, you can watch artisans ply their craft. This leather business blends seamlessly into the authenticity that runs throughout Blaauwklippen.

For a bite to eat, the coachman's lunch is a hearty meal. In the summer, sit outside on the stoep or in the garden at the back. The museum room in the tasting area provides a warm and homely ambience for winter lunches.

Blaauwklippen was one of the original land grants in the Stellenbosch area. This historic heritage has been preserved with integrity. Blaauwklippen offers many things to do and envelops your senses in a wholesome and genuine atmosphere.

On the slopes of Helshoogte ('hell's height') beneath the powerhouse of Groot Draken-stein ('great dragon rock') lies a small winery. With about five acres under vine Camberley produces no more than a thousand cases of wine neatly packaged in 500ml bottles. From their rich red soils they produce only one wine – a cabernet sauvignon touched with a bit of merlot.

The passion at Camberley shines through the wine and the winery. The Nels moved to Helshoogte in the early 1990s from Cape Town and planted vines. What was initially a devoted hobby has metamorphosed into a compelling lifestyle. The warm and optimistic approach at Camberley is welcoming and gracious.

While John Nel actively tends the vines and ardently creates the wine, Gaël (a talented caterer) runs the B&B – two separate and private cottages on the winery. Surrounding their elegant Victorian home are neat rows of vines and trim gardens flush with white roses. There is an artistic precision in the seemingly casual arrangement of plants that enhances the tranquillity of such a majestic setting.

The cellar, in fact, is part of the Nels' home. You're as likely to enter the tasting lounge from the kitchen as through the cellar door. Unlike many tasting centres, this one could be your family room. Above the cellar it has an open-plan kitchen, dining area and sitting room. Just beyond is a guest suite for those lucky enough to have booked a room. The walls are filled with interesting nostalgia – from a map of the world on an entire wall to various sports items. There are books of all kinds scattered about.

Tasting at Camberley is an animated conversation amongst friends. Johnny's broad grin and hearty enthusiasm are infectious. A stop at Camberley will certainly set you smiling.

Helshoogte Pass (R310)
Tel: (021) 885-1176

WINEMAKER: John Nel
OWNER: John and Gaël Nel

OPEN: 9–5 Mon to Sat
    preferably by appointment
CLOSED: 25 & 26 December, New Year's
    Day

TOURS: None
TASTINGS: No charge for individuals
WINES OFFERED FOR TASTING:
    Cabernet Sauvignon–Merlot

RESTAURANT: None
PICNICS: By prior arrangement
ACCOMMODATION: B&B

WHEELCHAIRS: No

An old faithful, continuing to produce top-class wines. Thirty years ago, you would have known their wines as Montagne, which included the fabulously drinkable cabernet blend.

As you drive past the vineyards, you can't help observing the red soil – it could almost be a pure pigment. Notice also the cabernet vines on the left and the shiraz on the right. Mind the speed bumps. They're serious about people driving slowly. The wetland gully between vineyards absolutely bursts with arum lilies in the winter. And look for the Cape pine with its branches spun about like the horses on a carousel.

There is a Dutch austerity to the historic buildings. The simple, sharp angles are softened by the rolling lawns and gardens. A gentle canopy of shade from the old oak trees surrounds the horseshoe-shaped terrace. The air is festive – whether you are on your own or with a crowd. It's as though you can hear the joyous spirit pervading Hartenberg.

This is a quiet and secluded estate, immensely appealing in its intimacy. The delicate scent of yesterday-today-and-tomorrow bushes floats past, mingled with the mimosa trees, jasmine and rosemary.

Though the manor house is private, the side angle of the gable and stoep is worth noting. The Calvinist style is quite different from that of most gables in the area. The house was rebuilt in the 1700s when an austere architecture was at its height. It is thought that the first house, dating back to the 1680s, sported Baroque detail but this legacy was destroyed by fire. The large stone slabs leading to the front door were salvaged from the vineyards. These have been identified as part of the original road from Stellenbosch to Table Bay, which passed through the farm. If you look carefully on the way out, the old stone road is discernible on the left just after the workers' cottages.

The tasting room is bright and open. On cold winter days, they stoke a roaring fire. The yellowwood tables and riempie chairs have that well-used but well-cared-for look. It's a very comfortable way to taste their wines. The tasting guides are well-informed professionals keen to make sure you have a special experience at Hartenberg.

Bottelary Road (M23)
Tel: (021) 882-2541
e-mail: hartenberg@cybertrade.co.za

WINEMAKER: Carl Schultz
OWNER: MacKenzie family

OPEN: 9–5 Mon to Fri; 9–3 Sat
CLOSED: Christmas, New Year's Day, Good Friday

TOURS: None
TASTINGS: Nominal charge, refundable with purchase
WINES OFFERED FOR TASTING: Sauvignon Blanc, Chardonnay, Weisser Riesling, Cabernet Sauvignon, Merlot, Pontac, Shiraz, Zinfandel, Red blends

RESTAURANT: None
PICNICS: Picnics in summer, pub lunches in winter

An interesting thing about Hazendal is that I haven't found their vineyards yet! I'm told that they are across the way. But that's not really important to the Hazendal experience. No matter where the vineyards are, the Hazendal Estate is a spectacular configuration of old Cape Dutch architecture. And the Russian objects inside are no less inspiring.

Hazendal was originally settled in 1699 by a German named Christoffel Hazenwinkel, from whom the estate took its name. The homestead gable is a magnificent example of High Baroque detail, sporting convex–concave scrolls like a sugar-plum fairy. This contrasts eloquently with the original wine cellar adjacent to the house and the simplicity of the slave quarters further to the right. The wine cellar is now a national monument and houses the wine-tasting centre. Its double-volume beam-and-thatch roof adds an element of space to the otherwise long and narrow building so typical of the early architecture.

Hazendal was reborn in the 1990s, when Russian-born Dr Mark Voloshin restored the estate to its elegant glory of centuries past. The tasting room reflects elements of his native country and his passion for things Russian. The cabinets display all kinds of vodka, many of which you will probably never have heard of before. In the loft, Fabergé eggs, ornaments and jewellery are displayed in glittering light. These can be admired and, with a bit of serious money, purchased. For those who take a tour, you will be treated to a trip through the Marvol Museum – a repository of Russian icons, paintings and a private collection of some particularly special Fabergé eggs.

At the end of the tasting room there is a large, circular fireplace. The comfortable, somewhat worn, over-stuffed chairs and ottomans are perfectly chosen and placed. The couches are draped with intricately designed tapestries. It all has the feeling of a cozy mountain lodge.

The peaceful restaurant is centred between the tasting room and the fermentation cellar, which can be viewed through walls of glass. The ceiling is painted in a traditional European style, depicting historical moments at the estate, the importance of the vineyards, and the coats of arms of the various owners through the centuries. There is also alfresco dining to the sides of the restaurant under the shade of vines.

Hazendal exudes a sense of refinement. It invites you to relax on comfortable sofas, to read interesting books and magazines, and to luxuriate in its peacefulness. It is elegant and well-heeled, without being pretentious.

Bottelary Road (M23)
Tel: (021) 903-5035
e-mail: info@hazendal.co.za

WINEMAKER: Ronell Wiid
OWNER: Dr Mark Voloshin

OPEN: 9–4:30 Mon to Fri;
10–3 Sat to Sun
CLOSED: Christmas, New Year's Day,
Good Friday

TOURS: 11 and 3. Nominal charge,
includes tasting
TASTINGS: No charge for individuals
WINES OFFERED FOR TASTING: Chenin
Blanc, Sauvignon Blanc, Chardonnay,
Shiraz–Cabernet Sauvignon blend,
Reserve red

RESTAURANT: Lunches, 12–2:30 Tues to
Sun
PICNICS: Available in summer

FESTIVALS & PROGRAMMES: Gourmet
evenings, art exhibitions

R44 North
(Stellenbosch-Paarl)
Tel: (021) 884-4656
e-mail: wine@kanonkop.co.za

WINEMAKER: Beyers Truter
OWNER: Johann and Paul Krige

OPEN: 8:30–5 Mon to Fri; 8:30–12:30 Sat
CLOSED: Christmas, New Year's Day,
    Good Friday

TOURS: By appointment
TASTINGS: No charge for individuals
WINES OFFERED FOR TASTING: Cabernet
    Sauvignon, Pinotage, Red blends

RESTAURANT: NONE
PICNICS: Not accommodated but will
    provide a braai for 15 or more by
    arrangement

Kanonkop means 'cannon hill'. The cannon on the entrance pillar tells the story. It was used as a form of signal to the farmers in the Stellenbosch area. When ships sailed into Table Bay a cannon was fired, announcing it was time for the farmers to load up produce, head for Cape Town and sell or barter their goods with the sea-weary visitors.

When you approach Kanonkop, the peaks of the Stellenbosch Mountains spike up behind the vines that cover the northern tail of the Simonsberg. Victorian street lamps and white rose bushes line the drive to the estate. As you turn into Kanonkop, a stream trickles under the weeping willows. A canopy of oak trees with huge trunks and high branches covers the parking area with much-appreciated shade. Kanonkop is a complex of family homes. The Georgian influence is notable in the strong, straight lines and whitewashed buildings under the oaks.

Wherever you see the word Kanonkop, read red wine and accolades. This estate has been showered with awards for so many years that they only display the most recent ones at the tasting centre. And not just from one judging panel, but from around the world: the UK, Asia, the United States, Europe, Australasia and, of course, South Africa. This singularly red estate is renowned for pinotage and a bordeaux blend, Paul Sauer: both great wines for cellaring. Take the Kadette if you're looking for something to open sooner.

The Paul Sauer blend is named after the family's father, who was an esteemed politician and cabinet minister of the Republic. It was Sauer's father, also a politician, who originally purchased the estate. In 1973 the first wines were made by Jan 'Boland' Coetzee and Jannie Krige, son-in-law of Paul Sauer. Jan 'Boland' has become a legend in South African wine history since the early years.

In 1980 Beyers Truter took over the winemaking reins from Jan 'Boland'. Truter has also become a highly rated winemaker, with *Wine Magazine* aptly dubbing him the 'King of Pinotage'. Jannie and Mary Krige's sons have taken over the management of the estate; this 'new' team has achieved consistently high marks and wide praise for their wines.

And for the tasting guests, Kanonkop is an absolute pleasure. The guides are unassuming and friendly. They're genuinely interested in your trip to the winelands, sharing information and suggesting places to see.

**R44 North
(Stellenbosch-Paarl)
Tel: (021) 884-4511
e-mail: info@laibach.co.za
www.laibach.co.za**

**WINEMAKER: Stefan Dorst
OWNER: Friedrich Laibach Family**

**OPEN: 9–5 Mon to Fri; 9–1 Sat
CLOSED: Christmas, Good Friday**

**TOURS: By appointment
TASTINGS: Nominal charge, refundable
   with purchase
WINES OFFERED FOR TASTING: Chenin
   Blanc, Sauvignon Blanc, Chardonnay,
   Cabernet Sauvignon, Pinotage,
   Cabernet Sauvignon–Merlot blend,
   Merlot, Sweet Natural**

**RESTAURANT: None
PICNICS: Picnic baskets in summer**

WHEELCHAIRS: No

Laibach has modern architecture and modern attitude. Sensitive to the graphic shapes of the environment, the long barrel roofs mirror the valley that forms at the winery's edge. The valley, almost like a chute, seems to extend to Table Mountain. Such a subtle play between the built and the natural environment embodies the appeal of this winery.

When you arrive, it's not quite clear where to park. But as long as it's not harvest season, it shouldn't particularly matter. The entrance is not the obvious barn door to the cellar but is elusively tucked away at the side, down the herb path.

With its brick, wood, terracotta and steel, Laibach is just short of modern industrial in style. The form and material capture the estate's proximity to the oceans – contemporary, cool lines accentuated with a touch of seaside wood.

On the inside, Laibach's setting is complemented by deep blues and crisp yellows. The paintings of grapes seem as though you could touch the must. Rock music plays in the background. It's young, trendy and exciting.

On the patio, relax and enjoy the rolling hills covered with vineyards. Or try the upstairs deck where you cantilever over the vines.

The estate was purchased in 1994 by the Laibach family from Germany. Their vision was to harness the character of the vineyards in an estate wine. Prior to their ownership, the grapes were sent to Nederburg where the individual character was lost, submerged in making a wine from no specific place. The new team at Laibach changed all that. With a great deal of focused energy they rooted the new cellar in the hillside. They then set about creating quality wines and have found themselves making a solid name for the estate.

**R44 North
(Stellenbosch-Paarl)
Tel: (021) 875-5226**

**WINEMAKER: James Farquharson
OWNER: Paul Benadé**

**OPEN: 9–5 Mon to Fri ; 9–1 Sat
CLOSED: Christmas, New Year's Day,
 Good Friday**

**TOURS: By appointment
TASTINGS: No charge for individuals
WINES OFFERED FOR TASTING:**
 Sauvignon Blanc, Chardonnay,
 Weisser Riesling, Cabernet
 Sauvignon, Shiraz, Red blends,
 Late Harvest

**RESTAURANT: None
PICNICS: Not accommodated**

Now *this* is like home. Comfy couches surround the fireplace, and the farm-style table is a place where you could sit down to a good conversation with interesting and unusual people from around the world. Lievland reminds me of Telluride. It's secluded and earthy with its own kind of flair. The people are warm and friendly. No designer slicks here; just a pair of good jeans, a bit of style and a laid-back attitude.

The road to Lievland is narrow, built on the edge of the mountainside. Vines have been planted on the steep upper slope. The trees and firs tower above. As you near the homesteads, the forest opens up to reveal a private valley with vines and marsh: a clearing you do not expect.

The tasting centre is in the elaborately gabled Cape Dutch thatch house dating from 1823. Set on the slopes of the hillside, it overlooks the wetland gully separating the folds in the mountain. In the summer and autumn, the marsh is filled with cat-tails, while in late winter and spring it is home to wild arum lilies.

It is easy for one to visualise the construction of original Cape homes from the tasting centre: a single building consisting of one long and narrow room, which was often divided into three parts. It was after the owners had the made their wealth that they extended the buildings and frequently added gables. In fact, many of the dates painted on homes around the Cape reflect the date when the gable was added rather than when the home was built. It is fairly common to find a difference of fifty years.

The tasting-centre gable is High Baroque. This ornate style was common at the time and, architecturally, reflects a period of affluence at the Cape.

To the left of the homestead is a neoclassically gabled manor house, in the main style prevailing after the Baroque period. The difference in styles is obvious: this is one of the few wineries where you can compare such good examples of each. The neoclassical gable has a simple, angular movement that relies on the lines to create a clean, crisp look. It is more Georgian in influence and reflects an abstinence rather than a Baroque opulence.

Before you leave, take note of some later additions. In front of the neoclassical manor house, there's a fabulously retro petrol pump. And wonder at the remarkable ways of nature – there is a huge, hollow oak tree that insists on growing.

LONGRIDGE WINERY

Eikendal Road off R44 South
(Stellenbosch–Somerset West)
Tel: (021) 855-2004

WINEMAKER: Ben Radford
OWNER: Trylogy Winecorp

OPEN: 9–5 Mon to Fri; 9–2 Sat
CLOSED: Christmas, Good Friday

TOURS: By appointment
TASTINGS: No charge for individuals
WINES OFFERED FOR TASTING:
  Sauvignon Blanc, Chenin Blanc,
  Chardonnay, Cabernet Sauvignon,
  Shiraz, Merlot, Pinotage, Red blends,
  Cap Classique

RESTAURANT: None
PICNICS: 24-hour notice required

The Eikendal Road is home to a trio of wineries, with Longridge the highest of these. A new estate, Longridge is built in the Cape Victorian vernacular: a long building with sash windows and a casual outdoor patio garden. The borders of the winding path to the tasting centre are grown with indigenous shrubs and plants. The view from Longridge is spectacular.

As part of a corporately owned complex of wineries, Longridge produces a sizeable quantity of wine from quaffers to show-stoppers. They are all made at the winery and a tour is easy to arrange. The cellar facilities are, however, located at the sister estate, Spier, which is also renowned for its amphitheatre where plays and concerts are performed.

Spier overflows with Cape Dutch architecture, rambling walks and several restaurants. Longridge, by comparison, is quiet. It offers the opportunity of personal interaction with the wine guides. The patio is a great place to take your own picnic and enjoy the sun and view with your wine. The lawn and vineyards in front of the building provide running space and a variety of interests for the young.

The tasting room is on the ground floor. Terracotta and wood predominate in this spacious room. Its cabinet-panelled walls display the extensive range of wines as well as those that the company imports. The appeal of Longridge is its casualness: no fancy talk, no wine-snob intimidation – a relaxed place to share a glass of wine with a few friends.

Meerlust is an icon in the Cape wine scene. Their wines have garnered award after award, year after year. You'll find Meerlust wines at the best restaurants and in the best cellars. If you are a wine enthusiast, Meerlust is inspiring.

You do not go to Meerlust to taste the wine and head for the next winery. You go for the special one-to-one experience with the winemaker. Or you can simply drop in to buy their wine. Meerlust is not a public winery, and you must make an appointment.

The winemaker, Giorgio Dalla Cia, is a sanguine Italian. He has been a part of Meerlust for over twenty years and he is thoroughly commanding. With three generations of winemakers as his heritage, his knowledge is almost intuitive. A true professional, he experimented for fourteen years with chardonnay before releasing the first bottle to the public. Dalla Cia focuses his talents on creating a few wines in classic French styles which are subtle and complex.

As you enter Meerlust, you sense the discipline. The spotlessness and efficient organisation are evident everywhere. The long brick drive through the vineyards is bordered alternately by palms and oak trees. It opens onto the gabled homestead with its vine-covered porch.

Behind the richly grained doors to the winery lies the tasting room, which is dimly lit and quite cool. The long, thick wooden table conjures up images of a monastery.

The barrel maturation cellar is across the courtyard. It is home to four vintages at any one time. Dalla Cia explains the difference between the various types of oak and the effect on the wines – little details like this enhance the experience. In contrast to the immaculate surroundings, the cellar walls are black with fungus. According to Dalla Cia, the walls are covered with a strain of penicillin that occurs spontaneously in the cellar. This penicillin thrives on other bacterial organisms and maintains the cleanliness of the cellar naturally.

The grappa distillery is housed in a small barn. A recent addition to Meerlust, it is a true boutique distillery. George Dalla Cia, Giorgio's son, exercises his artistry here. George takes you through the process with relish, providing interesting snippets that animate the process. The elegance of Meerlust grappa will convert many sceptics.

Meerlust is a private enclave for the family, not a showcase for the world. But they do share the cellars and distillery hospitably with you because that is what Meerlust is all about.

R310
Tel: (021) 843-3587
e-mail: meerlust@iafrica.com

WINEMAKER: Giorgio Dalla Cia
GRAPPA MAKER: George Dalla Cia
OWNER: Hannes Myburgh

OPEN: 8:30–5 Mon to Thur; 8:30–4:30
   Fri. By appointment for tastings
CLOSED: Public holidays. Between
   Christmas and New Year plus a few
   days on each side

TOURS: By appointment only
TASTINGS: Expensive, not refundable
WINES OFFERED FOR TASTING:
   Chardonnay, Merlot, Pinot Noir,
   Rubicon, Grappa

RESTAURANT: None
PICNICS: Not accommodated

MORGENHOF

A wonderfully restored estate, Morgenhof is a complex of country Cape Dutch buildings. Set amidst its rolling lawns are restaurants and picnic luncheon spots. Under the shade of oaks and plane trees, you can enjoy the Epicurean reputation that Morgenhof garnered from the start.

The estate was granted in 1692 but it was the Huchons, with their venerable Cointreau connection, who put Morgenhof amongst the ranks of the country's finest. Purchased in 1993, the estate underwent a massive renovation and replanting programme. This included the construction of a new underground barrel-maturation centre for the red wines. Holding up to 2000 small oak barrels, the cellar has octagonal dimensions and the barrels are set out in a circular form. This facilitates access and optimal efficiency.

Above ground and mirroring the vaulted cellar below, a rose and bush garden has been laid out in a classical style. This beautifully manicured garden is flanked by two new buildings, Le Tastevin and The Tower, which are undoubtedly inspired by the French château. Le Tastevin is used for private functions and formal tastings. Wedding receptions are frequently hosted at Morgenhof where the beautiful gardens add a magical touch.

From the observation gallery at The Tower, you can absorb the architectural splendour of the underground cellar. A separate maturation cellar has been created for the white wines, most notably the chenin blanc and chardonnay. This smaller cellar can be viewed from the tasting centre.

On the north-western haunch of the Simonsberg, Morgenhof hugs the mountain. The simple, farm style of the original Cape Dutch buildings lends a casual air.

Morgenhof is a positively professional estate. In the high summer season, the air is filled with chatter and laughter as people spill over the lawns. The lush vegetation, including ferns and bougainvillaea, provides a colourful foreground to the whitewashed buildings. In the winter, The Gazebo is warmed by the open fireplace, which fills the room with a quiet intimacy.

R44 North
(Stellenbosch-Paarl)
Tel: (021) 889-5510
e-mail: info@morgenhof.com
www.morgenhof.com

WINEMAKER: Rianie Strydom
OWNER: Anne Cointreau-Huchon

OPEN: Nov to Apr 9–5:30 Mon to Fri, 10–5 Sat to Sun; May to Oct 9–4:30 Mon to Fri, 10–3 Sat to Sun
CLOSED: Christmas, New Year's Day, Good Friday

TOURS: Scheduled tours at 11:00. Formal tastings and tour; cellar tours, nominal charges
TASTINGS: Nominal charges for tasting
WINES OFFERED FOR TASTING: Sauvignon Blanc, Chenin Blanc, Chardonnay, Cabernet Sauvignon, Merlot, Pinotage, Red blends

SHOP: Souvenirs
RESTAURANT: Summer in the garden, winter in The Gazebo
PICNICS: None

Rustic with a character all its own, Muratie is utterly charming. There is no way to create the fabulous, quirky ambience except through years of collecting a bit of this and a bit of that. The cobwebs are famous, the art of Georg Canitz renowned. Muratie's charm lies in its genuineness. It is not a glamorous showpiece fresh from a face-lift. Rather, it is weathered and full of character developed over years.

The winery is just discernible as a Victorian cottage. The corrugated-iron roof is rusted and patched and isn't really straight anymore. Everything has been built around the natural lie of the ground; even the cobblestones slope to and fro around the roots of the massive trees. The old farm implements haven't been put outside purely for decoration. You can imagine that when they weren't needed any longer, they were just moved out of the way – as far as the front porch. The old cellar is dark and almost musty. The small wooden tasting-counter serves maybe three or four people. The little room is cozy. Alcoves for seated tastings have been created from the old cement fermenting vats.

Besides being unusual, Muratie has a classic 300-year history, dating back to 1699. Reference to various aspects of its past can be found dotted about. The founder, Lourens Campher, married a freed slave, Ansela van de Caab. Today, a much-awarded red blend is named after her. Another owner, Georg Canitz, took up residence at Muratie in the early half of the 20th century. He was one of the best known South African artists in his day, and his work was collected as far afield as Europe and America. Many of his pieces grace Muratie's walls, forming an integral part of its character and appeal. Canitz gave more than art to Muratie; he also introduced the first pinot noir to South African soil. Muratie is still known for its deft handling of this delicate and fickle grape. The current owners, the Melck family, have returned to the estate once owned by their forebears. The Melcks have had a long and impressive influence on the Cape wine industry. At Muratie, they continue that tradition.

Before you leave, take a stroll to the garden: tables are scattered about the shaded lawn, next to the reflecting pool. Enjoy the tranquillity and the classic view of Table Mountain guarded by Lion's Head and Signal Hill.

R44 North
(Stellenbosch-Paarl)
Tel: (021) 882-2330
e-mail: muratie@kingsley.co.za

WINEMAKER: Mark Carmichael-Green
OWNER: Melck Family

OPEN: 9–5 Mon to Thur; 9–4 Fri; 9–3 Sat
CLOSED: Christmas, Good Friday

TOURS: By appointment
TASTINGS: Nominal charge
WINES OFFERED FOR TASTING: Pinot Noir, Cabernet Sauvignon–Merlot blend, Dessert wine and Port

SHOP: Souvenirs

RESTAURANT: By prior arrangement
PICNICS: By prior arrangement
ACCOMMODATION: Guest cottages

WHEELCHAIRS: No

REG VAN TOEGANG VOORBEHOU
RIGHT OF ADMISSION RESERVED

The Jonkershoek Valley is beguiling, so different from other parts of Stellenbosch. The mountains slice into the earth virtually at your feet as the valley narrows to the gorges in the mountain range. There is no thoroughfare.

In this valley, under the watchful towers of a flamboyant castle, rests the peaceful and urbane Neil Ellis winery. Sleek and refined, Neil Ellis winery is an understatement in sophistication. The quiet warmth of the sandstone walls and the horizontal symmetry extend throughout the winery, leaving one with a sense of peace. It is through simplicity that the graceful ambience is created. The gardens are a vast openness, lush with acres of grass and cooled by the immense pond. There is a harmony at Neil Ellis that is hard to find elsewhere.

Neil Ellis, the winemaker, has an immense stature in Cape wine circles, enjoying an illustrious career from the start. After spending several years as winemaker at Groot Constantia and then at Zevenwacht, he went on to establish his own winery in a unique manner. Credited with developing the first winery that had neither its own vineyards nor its own cellar, he pioneered the use of regional blocks for individual wines. Because there was not a winery in the traditional sense for many years, winemaking facilities being leased from other estates, there was no need to limit the vineyards geographically. There are vineyards in Elgin, Stellenbosch and Darling. The wines from the different regions are not blended. Rather, they are created separately to reflect their individual characteristics.

The new Neil Ellis winery reflects the ethos of his wines. There is a harmony in both the wines and the place.

Jonkershoek Rd
Tel: (021) 887-0649
e-mail: info@neilellis.com

WINEMAKER: Neil Ellis
OWNERS: Neil Ellis Wines (Pty) Ltd

OPEN: 9:30–4:30 Mon to Fri; 10–2 Sat
CLOSED: Christmas, Good Friday

TOURS: None
TASTINGS: No charge for individuals
WINES OFFERED FOR TASTING:
   Sauvignon Blanc, Chardonnay,
   Cabernet Sauvignon, Pinotage, Red
   blends

RESTAURANT: None
PICNICS: Not accommodated

Lemons, plums and a magnificent display of agapanthus greet you upon entering this 'gentleman's estate'. Rolling over the foothills of the Simonsberg, the estate tucks into the valleys and crests the slopes of the mountain. Oaks line the drive past herds of Jersey cattle and a stream guides you to the winery. It is verdant and pastoral, elegant and stately. Every detail has been attended to with great care.

The Rustenberg homesteads are truly spectacular examples of early Cape architecture. Amongst the first farms settled in Stellenbosch, the estate dates to 1682, when Roelof Pasman from Meurs, Germany, was amongst the first fifteen families to accept Simon van der Stel's offer of land in the newly proclaimed district. One of the many owners since then included John X. Merriman, Prime Minister of the Cape, from whom the current owners, the Barlows, acquired the farm. It was some years before the adjoining farm, Schoongezicht, could be reincorporated into the property after more than a hundred years. Rustenberg has an illustrious history, filled with famous characters and much passion.

The impressive new tasting centre is an elegant incorporation of the old Cape Dutch style with understated, modern sleekness. The combination of textures is complex and subtle with the use of worn brick, reflective metal, uneven slate, glass, smooth concrete pillars with rough blasted sections, and polished wood. There are undertones of a nautical theme in the oval gallery and curved staircase.

The main tasting counter is made from big barrels taken out of the old cellar. The serpentine design follows the flow of the tasting guests. There is no standing in queues or jostling for a position. The attention to detail and to their guests' comfort is yet again noticeable. Rustenberg is one of few estates to offer tasting in delicate crystal glasses. It is refreshing to be treated with the courtesy that acknowledges visitors won't break the glasses.

The sitting room off the end of the tasting room is almost like a state room on an elegant ship. The oversized sofas and chairs are a welcome respite, and they'll even offer you a cup of coffee or tea. In the winter, a fire warms the hearth. You'll want a good book, some good friends and an afternoon – you're not likely to leave too soon. In the summer, sit out in the courtyard surrounded by the historic buildings.

Helshoogte Pass (R310)
Tel: (021) 809-1200
e-mail: wine@rustenberg.co.za
www.rustenberg.co.za

WINEMAKER: Adi Badenhorst
OWNER: Simon Barlow

OPEN: 9–4:30 Mon to Fri; 9–12:30 Sat
CLOSED: Christmas, Good Friday

TOURS: By appointment
TASTINGS: No charge for individuals
WINES OFFERED FOR TASTING:
   Sauvignon Blanc, Chardonnay,
   Cabernet Sauvignon, Red blends, Port

RESTAURANT: None
PICNICS: Not accommodated

FESTIVALS & PROGRAMMES:
   4pm – milking Schoongezicht cows

Not surprisingly, you'll identify Stonewall by the stone wall surrounding the homestead ensemble of buildings. Set amid the vineyards, Stonewall stands out from its surroundings and from most wineries. It is not tucked away behind a hill or down a long, winding road. It is spread out next to the main thoroughfare. What always confounds me is how quiet it is once you're at the winery. The noise of the passing traffic disappears as you melt into the ambience of an historic Cape Dutch farmstead.

Stonewall has been in the family for generations. The manor house is a typical Cape Dutch homestead. Its beautiful gable dates from the late-17th century. Stonewall is a family home. You'll find kids and dogs frolicking about the lawns under the trees. You might also have to step aside for the occasional tractor roaming about.

The tasting room is in an old building, once the horse stables. The soft yellow walls are soothing and, being two feet thick, make the room cool all the year round. Notice that it still houses the original trough. The feeling is rustic with a simple warmth.

When we visited for the first time, Stonewall had just opened to the public. Much to our delight, we met the owner, De Waal Koch. The short time we spent with him was memorable. He was not afraid to think, to ask questions or to challenge industry practices. But he always remained polite.

Stonewall has two well-appointed rooms for bed and breakfast. Though also situated in the old building housing the tasting centre, the B&Bs are definitely separate and private. The rooms are comfortable with renovated, modern facilities. This is where you go if you want to get far away from anything resembling a hotel. You'll feel like you're part of the farm: truly sleeping amongst the vineyards.

R44 South
(Stellenbosch–Somerset West)
Tel: (021) 855-3675

WINEMAKER: Martin Meinert
OWNER: De Waal Koch

OPEN: 9–5 Mon to Fri; 9–1 Sat
CLOSED: Christmas, Good Friday

TOURS: By appointment
TASTINGS: No charge for individuals
WINES OFFERED FOR TASTING:
 Sauvignon Blanc, Chenin Blanc,
 Chardonnay, Cabernet Sauvignon,
 Red blend

RESTAURANT : None
PICNICS: Light meals with 24-hour
 notice
ACCOMMODATION: B&B

Most of us will instantly recognise Thelema. The label is one of the most widely known of all South African wines throughout the world. A bold statement maybe, but the wines are often sold out soon after they have been released.

The first time I walked into Thelema, I was immediately struck by its cathedral atmosphere: a sense of space and light and openness. A commitment that borders on spiritual passion pulsates soothingly throughout the winery. The Simonsberg and Drakenstein mountains, sometimes dusted in snow, tower outside the double-volume windows.

Many years later I was to find out the origins of the name Thelema. It was not surprising that Thelema was a religious order – of sorts, that is. The fountainhead for the name was a story in *Gargantua and Pantagruel* by Rabelais. A French Franciscan monk, writer and poet in the 16th century, Rabelais is known for his vivid and often bawdy tales. An episode in the epic *Gargantua and Pantagruel* describes the founding of the Abbey of Thelema. Unlike religious orders of the day, Thelema was open to all men and women, noble and fair. Thelema was a place where human virtues were cultivated. Thelemites explored the delights and riches of Man and Nature. They pursued the essence of their true selves and personal wills. Still today Thelemites believe in absolute freedom and individuality.

Thelema is a fitting name for this winery. An icon in the South African wine industry, Gyles Webb has consistently produced outstanding wines. He was at the forefront of changing the environment, pushing the limits and winning. He has created his own freedom and developed his own individual style, and he is still challenging the limits.

Helshoogte Pass (R310)
Tel: (021) 885-1924
e-mail: thelema@adept.co.za

WINEMAKER: Gyles Webb
OWNERS: McLean Family & Gyles Webb

OPEN: 9–5 Mon to Fri; 9–1 Sat
CLOSED: Public holidays

TOURS: By appointment
TASTINGS: No charge for individuals
WINES OFFERED FOR TASTING:
    Sauvignon Blanc, Chardonnay, Rhine
    Riesling, Muscat de Frontignan,
    Cabernet Sauvignon, Merlot,
    Pinotage, Late Harvest

SHOP: Souvenirs
RESTAURANT: None
PICNICS: Not accommodated

A seemingly endless variety of proteas lines the drive to Verdun, and a grove of old palm trees greets you on your arrival. Behind them is an equally old Victorian farmhouse, complete with a tin roof and large porch, and surrounded by cabbage patches and bougainvillaea. Imagine Auntie Mame gliding out of the french doors to offer a welcoming mint julep.

The tasting centre is further along and has a more Californian feel to it – sort of an *en piste* day lodge on the slopes of Tahoe, without the snow. The downhill run is the flight of steps leading from the parking area to the fountain and gardens. A breezy space with glass all round, there is little distinction between the inside and the casual deck extending to the dam. The whole area is filled with wooden tables that look out over the water to the Helderberg and Stellenbosch Mountains.

An ancient name, Verdun has roots in France. The fortified town on the banks of the River Meuse gave its name to the Treaty of Verdun, which was signed in AD 843. This agreement between the three grandsons of Charlemagne divided his empire among them. The East Kingdom later became Germany; the West Kingdom, France; and the Middle Kingdom became known as the Low Countries, Lorraine, Burgundy and Northern Italy.

Our local Verdun has roots that go back to the early days of the Cape. More recently, Verdun was a popular jaunt in the 1970s. But it went through a down time. The buildings weren't maintained, nor were the cellar facilities. As it became more dilapidated, the winery fell off the list of places to go. They stopped making wine at the estate and it faded ever further into oblivion – that is, until François Tolken bought the challenge in the mid-nineties. Refurbished, cleaned up and renovated with new cellars, tasting facilities and vineyards, Verdun is firmly back on the map of places to go. And their wines are drawing the crowds too.

Polkadraai Road (M12)
Tel: (021) 886-5884
e-mail: verdunestate@verdun.co.za

WINEMAKER: Jan van Rooyen
OWNER: Tolken Family

OPEN: 9–5 Mon to Fri; 9–1 Sat
CLOSED: Christmas, Good Friday

TOURS: By appointment
TASTINGS: Moderate charge, refundable
   with purchase
WINES OFFERED FOR TASTING:
   Sauvignon Blanc, Chenin Blanc,
   Chardonnay, Gamay Noir, Merlot,
   Cabernet Sauvignon, Red blend

RESTAURANT: None
PICNICS: Bring your own and sit under
   the oaks at the dam

Vergelegen has always been about gardens. Forests and brooks border the expansive lawns. The rose garden envelops your senses. The symmetrical koi ponds mirror the balance of the library building. The herb garden is sensually delightful. The octagonal garden is a blush of colour all year round. The reflecting pool unites the tea garden with the manor house. All the gardens manifest a design precision and symmetry that is classical and beautiful. Vergelegen is more of an outing than a quick wine tasting.

From the time that the 400 morgen were granted to Willem Adriaan van der Stel in 1700, Vergelegen was destined to be a model estate based on the grand gardens of European royalty. An agricultural philosopher, Willem Adriaan wrote an extensively detailed *Gardener's Almanac*. At Vergelegen, he brought his vision to life. What remains of his original plantings are five 300-year-old Chinese camphor trees in front of the manor house.

Willem Adriaan van der Stel was the son of Simon van der Stel. The Dutch East India Company appointed him Governor after his father retired. Having spent the previous fifteen years in Holland, Willem Adriaan had been greatly influenced by the royal courts and their vast, orderly gardens. He brought this vision to Vergelegen.

Vergelegen is serene. There are no crowds packing through the manor house, browsing in the library, or jostling on the pathways. There is calmness, a freedom to meander about – on or off the pathways. The lawns are manicured. The mature trees tower above. Flowers carpet the ground under the cloak of shade. The buildings are beautifully restored, their detailing fine and considered. As you amble through the buildings and around the gardens, you feel as though you should be in period costume, talking to kings.

At the same time Vergelegen is exceptionally friendly for children. This is also the only estate to offer regular, guided farm walks. The groups are small and it is an enjoyable way to start the day, followed by breakfast at the Lady Phillips Tea Garden.

For a tour of the winery, you'll be ferried to the new cellar cresting a nearby hill. Overlooking the Peninsula, the views are magnificent.

Lourensford Road, Somerset West
Tel: (021) 847-13344

WINEMAKER: André van Rensburg
OWNER: Anglo American Farms

OPEN: 9:30–4 Mon to Sun
CLOSED: Christmas, New Year, Good Friday and Workers' Day

TOURS: Nominal entrance fee includes winery tour and tasting
May to Oct, 10 and 11 Mon to Sat;
Nov to Apr, 10, 11 and 3 Mon–Sat, 10 and 11 Sun
TASTINGS: Included in entrance fee
WINES OFFERED FOR TASTING:
Sauvignon Blanc, Chenin Blanc, Chardonnay, Gamay Noir

SHOP: Souvenirs
RESTAURANT: 847-1346, Lady Phillips Tea Garden, Rose Terrace
PICNICS: Not accommodated

FESTIVALS & PROGRAMMES: Guided farm walks 8:30–10 Tues and Sat, book at 847-1346

First a rugby legend, now a wine legend, Jan 'Boland' Coetzee made a name for himself early in his career as a winemaker. He worked wonders at Kanonkop for close to a decade. He continued to create miracles after he bought his own place, Vriesenhof. He is a consultant to a number of exclusive estates, some of which even make their wine at his cellars.

A classic Cape Dutch farm, Vriesenhof is special. It's both a home and a farm – gloriously reminiscent of a gentlemanly era of farming that is long gone. The gracious homestead is stately with its whitewashed walls, thatch roof and wooden shutters.

As we meandered through the cellars and over the pipes, I began to wonder whether we were going to be asked to help with an odd job or something. We had been warned that they were short of hands that day. Winding our way to the mysterious depths of the cellar was my idea of an exciting tasting experience. But more exciting was the tasting room.

Dimly lit by a single wall sconce and candles on the railway-sleeper table, I gasped when we walked into the room. Neither exotic nor overdone, there was actually not a single aspect that caught my attention. I've traced my reaction to the mood – the mood of the room, that is; an intimate room, with a roaring fire, an overstuffed sofa and a coffee table strewn with magazines. There would be no large groups here. I decided instantly that I was not leaving.

Jan's daughter placed all the bottles on the table with an army of glasses and apologised that she had to dash into town. 'Would we be all right on our own for a little while?' It was sheer magic – like a private tasting in your own home.

We did eventually leave, grudgingly perhaps but elated at our 'find'. Jan's son helped us load the wines into our car and we headed back to Stellenbosch. As we drove through the suburbs abutting the farm, Vriesenhof took on mythical proportions. The impressions have not changed over time. Only, now, the tasting room is near the entrance in the cellar. Vriesenhof remains legendary – like its owner.

Paradyskloof Road (off R44 South)
Tel: (021) 880-0284

WINEMAKER: Jan 'Boland' Coetzee
OWNER: Jan 'Boland' Coetzee

OPEN: 8:30–1, 2–5 Mon to Thur and
8:30–1, 2–4 Friday
CLOSED: Christmas, Good Friday

TOURS: By appointment
TASTINGS: No charge for individuals
WINES OFFERED FOR TASTING:
Sauvignon Blanc, Chardonnay,
Cabernet Sauvignon, Pinotage, Red
blends

RESTAURANT: None
PICNICS: Not accommodated

Exuberant and lively, Warwick has never stopped to question the trail it blazed. To its pioneering spirit, Warwick has held fast.

A genteel country farm, Warwick has an immediate, happy feel. When you meander onto the estate, the tall grass waves as the wind blows through the valley. A simple white fence corrals the low-lying field. On the other side of the brick-cobbled drive, the fruit trees are tall and flush with their bounty. In the winter, their silhouettes carve a sculptured web, complex in design, simple in striking contrast.

The oak and fir trees jostle for position along the drive towards the tasting room. The luxuriant orchard gives way to a garden of varied flowers hiding the main house. The trim farm buildings are crisp in their whiteness, while the banks of the stone waterway are rich in greenery with a display of mini-agapanthus, ferns and ivy. The terrace beckons you to enjoy a festive respite in the shade of the oaks. Inside is the tasting room. Opening out to the deck and beyond, the bucolic view is replete with cows meandering around the dam; above are the vineyards and beyond the distant image of Table Mountain.

Tuscan in its combination of rustic and refined elements, the tasting room is filled with gaiety. One would expect a large family to gather here for meals and laughter. There will be no large tours, no standing in front of a counter. Rather, you join in the carefree company of those who have mustered round a table-for-ten under the barrel-arched bamboo ceiling. The tasting leader is accomplished. And, typical of the estate, the discussion is sensible and plain-spoken. The talk flows with the interests of the visitors. There is something for novices and professionals, with descriptions of the tastes and textures and an emphasis on pairing the wines with food and when best to drink them.

The Warwick emblem is an ingenious chalice shaped as a woman holding a bowl above her head. When turned upside-down, the skirt becomes the goblet and the bowl swivels so that it may also be filled with the delights of Bacchus. The witty amusement is that the contents of both bowls must be consumed before the cup can be put down. A clever design indeed. And on the rosé label, the lady lets loose with a bit of hip-wagging frivolity!

R44 North
(Stellenbosch-Paarl)
Tel: (021) 884-4410
e-mail: ratcliffe@warwickwine.co.za
www: warwickwine.co.za

WINEMAKERS: Anna-Mariè Mostert &
Norma Ratcliffe
OWNER: Stan Ratcliffe

OPEN: 8:30–4:30 Mon to Fri,
by appointment on Sat
CLOSED: Public holidays

TOURS: By appointment
TASTINGS: No charge for individuals
WINES OFFERED FOR TASTING:
Chardonnay, Cabernet Sauvignon,
Cabernet Franc, Merlot, Pinotage,
Red blends

SHOP: Souvenirs
RESTAURANT: None
PICNICS: Not accommodated

Take a drive up to the lookout point for a 360° view: Robben Island, Table Mountain, Cape Point, False Bay, Drakenstein Mountains, Ceres Mountains, Paarl Rock, the Swartland. Overwhelming!

Developed by Cape Town architect Gilbert Colyn, Zevenwacht was the first Cape wine estate to issue shares to the public. The expansive vision required more funding than anticipated, culminating in its purchase by a private consortium. The Johnsons subsequently bought the estate. The initial vision continues to be developed with conference facilities, a heliport, holiday chalets, a 4x4 trail and a professional chefs' school.

Just as you can see everything, so you can do everything at Zevenwacht. It has created an environment for everyone. There is a Kiddies Corner playground, with swings and jungle gyms and hills to roll down; a fishermen's grotto; braai areas all round; picnic spots everywhere you turn: all to give you magical settings where you don't feel that everyone else has come to join you. Privacy without solitude.

There are pine forests and woodland surrounds. Buy picnic lunches at the alfresco counter and sit under the thatched boma, on the lawns or at the numerous tables dotted around. Many of the lunch ingredients are grown on the farm. In the mornings you can watch them pick for the day's meals. The historic homestead, with its beautiful Rococo gable, has been turned into a restaurant. Cool in summer, cozy in winter, it overlooks the reservoir and has a view towards Simon's Town.

The gardens are attractive and varied in an English sort of way – tended but on the verge of becoming overgrown. Even though the Zevenwacht complex is large, it maintains a comfortable and casual appeal. As it is one of only a few farms that also have a cheesery, don't miss their creamy and mature offerings as well as their extensive range of wines. The wine-tasting venue is well organised. It has a warm coziness even though it can accommodate lots of people.

It can be tricky getting to Zevenwacht, but persevere. As it is located at the end of Langverwacht Road, off the R102, you can reach it by the R300 or the Bottelary Road (M23) or from the Polkadraai Road (M12). I suggest following the Polkadraai Road. Whichever way, take a detailed road map with you.

Langverwacht Rd off R102
Tel: (021) 903-5123
e-mail: info@zevenwacht.co.za
www.zevenwacht.co.za

WINEMAKER: Hilko Hegewisch
OWNERS: Harold & Denise Johnson

OPEN: 8–5 Mon to Fri; 9:30–5 Sat & Sun;
 9:30–5 Public holidays
CLOSED: Christmas

TOURS: By appointment
TASTINGS: No charge for individuals
WINES OFFERED FOR TASTING:
 Sauvignon Blanc, Chenin Blanc,
 Chardonnay, Rhine Riesling, Cabernet
 Sauvignon, Shiraz, Pinotage, Red
 blends

SHOP: Souvenirs
RESTAURANT: Daily – breakfast, lunch
 and dinner
PICNICS: Baskets supplied by estate
ACCOMMODATION: Yes

Franschhoek

In the late 17th century, religious fanaticism was rife in Europe. The Edict of Nantes was repealed by King Louis XIV in 1685, marking an end to 87 years of religious freedom. The French Protestants were forced either to convert to Catholicism or to flee. Many chose to leave. Holland, tolerant even in those days, readily accepted these persecuted refugees. The Dutch East India Company offered them grants of land and a new life in the Cape. Most of the new settlers arrived between 1688 and 1700.

For Simon van der Stel, the Huguenots presented an opportunity to expand the Cape's territories as well as to improve the pool of wine-growing skills. Unlike the Dutch settlers, the Huguenots had experience in making wine. If they did not own wine farms in France, most had close relatives who were wine farmers. The immigrants were granted land on the other side of the Stellenbosch Mountains in the Drakenstein Valley. The area once known as Elephants' Corner became known as Le Quartier Français ('the French quarter'), which was later modified to Franschhoek ('French corner'). In a short time, the Huguenots turned the fertile soils of the Franschhoek Valley into green vineyards.

The graceful arches of the Huguenot Monument stand prominently at the end of town, commemorating the freedom of religious belief. For those wanting a bit of history about the village and the first settlers, head to the museum next door.

Over the years, Franschhoek's fields were variously planted with deciduous and citrus fruit or with wine grapes. The demand from the European market or devastation from disease was the deciding factor. The last great change-over to fruit occurred in the early part of the 20th century, when phylloxera had wiped out the vineyards. Combined with England's repeal of its tax on European wines, the effects decimated the farmers' fortunes. Vines were ripped out and the locals took to making preserves. Although wine continued to be made in the valley, it was not on the same scale.

A picturesque village, Franschhoek retains pride of place as the focal tourist destination in the winelands. In the past Capetonians used to visit for weekends in the winter, enjoying the warmer, sunnier days. Many wealthier families bought small farms for retreats, occasionally toying with winemaking. The general view held sway, however, that Stellenbosch was the area for serious wine growers. That is, until recently. The once-playful interest in winemaking has yielded to seriousness – with results that continue to

astound. The many folds in the mountains and the degree of slope offer a variety of growing conditions suitable for all types of grapes – even the super-sensitive pinot noir. It is partly in response to this opportunity and challenge that we are now witnesses to another great change-over: back to vineyards.

There is a certain sophistication about Franschhoek. A quiet village centred on three kilometres of the main road, it bustles with restaurants, cafés, art galleries, curios and boutique shops. The town attracts the glitterati and cognoscenti. Besides its sheer beauty and quaintness, Franschhoek exudes an elegance and understated gentility, all cloaked in the warmth and genuineness of the farming community which it is.

The scenery is dramatic: you've gone as far as you can and the mountains have buckled around you.

Boekenhoutskloof has a magical quality. It's like walking into a fairytale. Tucked into this corner of the Franschhoek Mountains is a peaceful haven of green lawns shaded by large oak trees. Sitting on the veranda of the farmhouse, you feel at home enjoying exquisite wines amongst friends. You may be discussing current affairs, which somehow seem so distant, or contemplating the serenity of the estate. Whatever the conversation, or lack of it, Boekenhoutskloof is definitely a place one does not want to leave.

The winery is new in the Franschhoek Valley. The farm was once a fruit farm until a partnership of seven purchased it with the intention of turning it into a world-class wine estate. It seems it was easier to make award-winning wine than to decide on the label. In the end, however, consensus was reached: seven Cape chairs in a row, each a different style, each uniquely crafted in the Cape from indigenous wood. There is the Tulbagh chair, the 'split-splat' chair, the Regency chair, the riempie chair, all made from local beechwood, yellowwood and stinkwood. Beechwood is common to the area and grows wild in the gorges and mountain forests on the farm. In fact, the winery's name, Boekenhoutskloof, means 'beechwood gorge'. The chairs on the label are typical of the styles made by the original settlers and, of course, there is one chair per partner.

As with fine cabinet work, the quality and attention to detail are evident throughout the winery's business, from the grape-selection table in the winery right down to the individually torn labels and the attractive boxes. The face of the partnership and driving force of the winery is Marc Kent, the winemaker. His laid-back style belies the activity and energy needed to make Boekenhoutskloof an estate of note. His easy style is peppered with acute and interesting insights. Marc prefers to meet each visitor to the winery and, more than offering you to taste the wines, he seems to share them.

Verdun Road
Tel: (021) 876-3320
e-mail: boeken@mweb.co.za

WINEMAKERS: Marc Kent
OWNER: Boekenhoutskloof Investments

OPEN: By appointment
CLOSED: Public holidays

TOURS: By appointment
TASTINGS: No charge
WINES OFFERED FOR TASTING:
   Sauvignon Blanc, Sémillon, Cabernet
   Sauvignon, Shiraz, Merlot

RESTAURANT: None
PICNICS: Not accommodated

BOSCHENDAL

Helshoogte Pass, R310 near R45
Tel: (021) 870-4000

WINEMAKER: JC Bekker
OWNER: Anglo American Corp

OPEN: Nov to Apr 8:30–4:30 Mon to Sat,
9:30–12:30 Sun; May to Oct 8:30–4:30
Mon to Fri, 8:30–1 Sat
CLOSED: Christmas, Good Friday

TOURS: By appointment, in summer only
874-1034
TASTINGS: No charge for individuals
WINES OFFERED FOR TASTING:
Sauvignon Blanc, Sémillon,
Chardonnay, Rhine Riesling, Cabernet
Sauvignon, Shiraz, Red blend

SHOP: Souvenirs
RESTAURANT: Le Café for light lunches
PICNICS: Le Pique-Nique (Nov to Apr)
reservations required for hampers

FESTIVALS & PROGRAMMES: Moonlight
picnics, March; Bastille Day, July

One of the grandes dames, guarded by the Groot Drakenstein and Simonsberg, Boschendal offers a little something to everyone: historic buildings, furnished manor house, picnic grounds, restaurants, ducks, geese and all manner of flowers, including the vast blush of fuchsia-coloured wild clover in winter.

Boschendal was granted to Jean le Long in 1685. But it was during the 160-year reign of the De Villiers family, who purchased Boschendal in 1712, that the estate reached its pinnacle. As with other old-family wine farms in the late 19th century, the De Villierses were forced to sell Boschendal. They remained wine farmers, purchasing other properties in the area, and their name is still found at places like Villiera and Mont Rochelle.

The Boschendal Estate is beautifully tended. The winter months are quieter and provide ample opportunity to absorb the splendours of this model estate. The summer is filled with the buzz of people cascading onto the lawns.

Boschendal is separated into two parts: the winery and tasting area, and the historic manor house and gardens, including the restaurants. Both are worth discovering. The vineyard tour is one of the better ones to book. They don't take tour groups, which means a more personal interaction with the guide. A self-guided tour of the exhibition vineyard is fascinating in summer, when you can distinguish between the varieties and compare the differences in the grapes and leaves and vines. A description sheet is provided to help you along!

On the other side of the estate, the manor house has been exquisitely refurbished. The rooms and artefacts are well detailed, and social commentaries are provided. While Boschendal had been a wine farm since the Huguenots arrived in 1685, it wasn't until 1812 that the manor house was completed. The classical styling of the homestead, with its jagged gables and urns, has graced many articles and books. With the vineyards in the foreground, the *werf* wall delineating the homestead grounds, and the mauve powerhouse of the Groot Drakenstein towering in the background, the picture is complete.

Situated at the entrance to the estate, the ample picnic grounds lure those who have the foresight to make reservations. Le Pique-Nique is a popular setting for lunch – and so it should be, with delicacies such as duck pâté, baguettes and caviar. This is no ordinary picnic under the oaks.

CABRIÈRE ESTATE

Berg Street
Tel: (021) 876-2630
e-mail: cabriere@iafrica.com

WINEMAKER: Achim von Arnim
OWNER: Clos Cabrière (Pty) Ltd

OPEN: 9–1, 2–4:30 Mon to Fri; 11–1 Sat.
   Tastings daily at 11 and 3
CLOSED: Christmas, Good Friday

TOURS: Saturday at 11, otherwise by
   appointment
TASTINGS: Moderate charges at
   appointed times
WINES OFFERED FOR TASTING: Pinot
   Noir, Chardonnay–Pinot Noir, various
   Cap Classiques, Ratafia (aperitif),
   Fine (brandy)

RESTAURANT: 876-3688 Haute Cabrière
   at the Cellar
PICNICS: Not accommodated

FESTIVALS & PROGRAMMES: Sabrage
   demonstration every Saturday tour or
   by prior arrangement

Baron Achim von Arnim, the inimitable host of Cabrière, energetically treats visitors to a display of *sabrage* on the Saturday morning tour. *Sabrage* is the feat of slicing a champagne bottle open with a sabre sword. With elegancy and flair, Achim enthrals visitors. He is a natural storyteller, and many visitors return regularly for the colourful show.

Cabrière specialises in *méthode champenoise*, or, as it is called in South Africa, *méthode cap classique*. In a lobster-for-champagne deal with France in 1992, South Africa agreed to change the name used for its champagne wines. Cabrière bottles its bubbly under the name of Pierre Jourdan and its still wine under Haute Cabrière.

Cabrière is a small estate located in the heart of the Franschhoek village. At the end of town, just before the T-junction at the Huguenot Monument, you turn right (south). Because you drive through the fields of a fruit farm to reach the estate, please respect the neighbours and drive slowly. The tastings are in a simple house filled with historic pieces. The guide explains each in turn, taking you on a journey through time while you sip champagne and learn about the process to create it.

Von Arnim's philosophy revolves around the sun, vine, soil and man. Each is crucial to survival and each is necessary to create the joys of Dionysian delights. You will find sundials and references to this fundamental belief at the estate as well as at the cellar. Located on the other side of the valley, on the Villiersdorp Pass road, the gravity-fed cellar has been sunk into the mountainside and covered with indigenous fynbos. The only tell-tale sign of its presence is the slight mound and the cars parked on the side. But beware, if you're the first to arrive, look for the signpost because you're likely to drive right past.

In line with his philosophy that wine and food are entwined, Von Arnim created the renowned restaurant, Haute Cabrière, in the estate's cellar on the hillside overlooking Franschhoek. This is a partnership with chef Matthew Gordon, who continues to create award-winning meals.

There are lovely views from the cool, cave-like building. The soaring, vaulted cellar seems to reach up from the depths of the mountain. When you view the cave from the dining area, it's as though you have discovered a hidden treasure trove or a secret access to faraway places. The single painting by Arabella Caccia adds the finishing touch to the restaurant, where there is also a large fireplace to warm the crisp winter days.

DIEU DONNÉ VINEYARDS

High on the south-westerly slopes to the north of Franschhoek village, Dieu Donné is tucked behind a hill. A short walk up the hill and you will find a beautiful setting to spread your picnic or share some wine. From there you take in the entire Franschhoek Valley and mountains: a true reflection of the estate's name, which translates as 'a gift from God'.

Dieu Donné was purchased by the Mauritian businessman Robert Maingard in the mid-1980s. The winery complex was created to blend in with the history of the Huguenot Valley. The buildings look like various old sheds or barns used centuries ago. Dieu Donné is not a fancy winery. It doesn't have elegant, commodious facilities. Its focus has been to create award-winning, affordable wines. And the walls are covered with the awards garnered over the years. The tasting area is a characterful room in the winery, where visitors share space with the admin office. You're there, in the thick of it. The tasting room is down the stairs under the shade trees. Be sure to take a jacket: it is a cool room – even in summer.

Dieu Donné is decidedly high up on the Franschhoek Mountains. It's as though the vines have been planted in the granite face of the mountain. In fact, Dieu Donné has a soil structure unique in the Franschhoek Valley. With the folds in the mountain, different layers or strata dominate in different blocks. This enables Dieu Donné to grow several noble varieties in optimal conditions.

You can experience some wonderful conversations about the wines, the soil (there are even samples of Hutton and Clovelly soils on the tasting counter), the rains and the mountain fires. If you're not sure where to go next, or where to have lunch, don't worry, your hosts would love to help you decide, suggesting various options depending on what it is that you are looking for. They truly want visitors to enjoy the winelands they are so passionate about.

The winemaker, Stephan du Toit, is overseeing some vast expansion programmes, which will increase production at this boutique to about 40 000 cases. Reserved, but with a vision, Stephan can sometimes be seen slipping into the admin area. He shares his office with 10 000 cases somewhere around the corner.

Uitkyk Road
Tel: (021) 876-2493
e-mail: dieudonn@zsd.co.za

WINEMAKER: Stephan du Toit
OWNER: Maingard family

OPEN: 9–5 Mon to Fri; Dec to Feb
9:30–12:30 Sat
CLOSED: Public holidays

TOURS: By appointment
TASTINGS: No charge for individuals
WINES OFFERED FOR TASTING:
Sauvignon Blanc, Chardonnay,
Cabernet Sauvignon, Merlot,
Pinotage, Late Harvest

RESTAURANT : None
PICNICS: Bring your own and sit atop the
hill overlooking the Franschhoek
Valley

High on the mountain slopes, Mont Rochelle looks north over the Franschhoek Valley. The vine-covered porch is a quiet place to enjoy lunch and relax with a glass of wine. It feels as if the place belongs to you. The views are exquisite. You'll want to linger for a while.

Mont Rochelle is one of the oldest farms in the valley. The original farm and homestead date back several centuries. Its past owners were many and, like all farms in the area, it was divided and consolidated over the years.

In the early 1990s, Graham and Lyn de Villiers acquired the farm and named it Mont Rochelle. The name is a dedication to Graham's heritage. In 1689, three De Villiers brothers from La Rochelle, France, fled persecution following the repeal of the Edict of Nantes. Under the auspices of the Dutch East India Company, they arrived at the Cape with letters of recommendation, acknowledging their winemaking skills, and were granted land in the Franschhoek Valley, which they named Mont Rochelle. While his own farm was not part of their land grant, Graham de Villiers can trace his roots to these brothers.

The tasting centre is in a homestead, probably a *jonkershuis*. Old oak trees flank the centre and the winery. Plum groves line the gentle slope below. The equestrian centre lies to the west just past the manor house, which is a magnificent example of Cape Dutch architecture. The private gardens are stunning in their classical design and supply another touch from the family's French heritage.

The atmosphere is friendly and helpful. The natural warmth from the wood extends the warmth of the people. Draw up a stool to the bar counter and enjoy their wonderful wines. It is such a relaxed environment that every time I've been there, other guests start talking to each other about the qualities of the wine, or where to stay or to eat lunch or to visit next. Mont Rochelle seems to have the special quality that makes everyone friends.

Dassenberg Rd off Reservoir West
Tel: (021) 876-3000
e-mail: montrochelle@wine.co.za

WINEMAKER: Justin Hoy
OWNER: Graham & Lyn de Villiers

OPEN: 11–4 Mon to Sat,
**   Sept to Apr 11–1 Sun**
CLOSED: Christmas, Good Friday

TOURS: 11:00, 12:30, 3:00 Mon to Fri,
**   nominal charge includes tasting fee**
TASTINGS: Nominal charge, refundable
**   with purchase, except for groups**
**   larger than 10**
WINES OFFERED FOR TASTING:
**   Sauvignon Blanc, Chardonnay,**
**   Cabernet Sauvignon, Merlot**

RESTAURANT: None
PICNICS: Light lunches year round 12–2
**   Mon to Sat; 12–1 Sun by prior**
**   arrangement**

Happy Valley Road
Tel: (021) 876-3055
e-mail: sales@moreson.co.za
    sales@pinehurst.co.za

WINEMAKER: Pierre Wahl
OWNER: Richard Friedman
MANAGER: Anton Beukes
SALES/MARKETING: Uschi van Zweel

OPEN: 11–5 Wed to Sun
CLOSED: Christmas

TOURS: By appointment
TASTINGS: Nominal charge
WINES OFFERED FOR TASTING:
    Sauvignon Blanc, Chardonnay,
    Cabernet Sauvignon, Merlot, Shiraz,
    Pinotage, Cap Classiques

RESTAURANT: Bread & Wine
PICNICS: Not accommodated

FESTIVALS & PROGRAMMES: Blessing of
    the Harvest Festival, February

Môreson means 'morning sun'. Situated in the valley, it is among the first to get the morning rays. The light bounces gently off the dew and the scent of lemon hangs in the air, letting you in on the secret about the other half of the farming operations.

Môreson was part of the original land grant, La Motte, back in 1695. This large tract was portioned many times. There were many different owners, sometimes consolidating portions, at other times splitting them up further. In the mid-1980s, the Friedman family purchased Môreson – Soleil du Matin.

A vibrant newcomer to the winelands, the Friedman family approached Môreson as a big business, even though this is a niche, boutique winery. Behind the public area of the complex is the heart of the operation. It buzzes with activity, marketing, farming, advertising, expansion, exporting, new wines. And yet it is all tightly structured and focused: no uncontrolled chaos here.

When the Friedmans began at Môreson, the wines were made at the Franschhoek Co-op. In the early 1990s, they built their own facilities and vinified their first wine in 1994. They have been building a solid name for their wines ever since, taking awards locally and internationally.

The wine-tasting area is a pleasant sienna-and-terracotta-styled room adjacent to the new winery. It continues the Mediterranean feel about the farm. The staff are helpful and well informed. Môreson maintains an extensive database of their customers, which they use for feedback and to introduce new vintages. Don't be shy to sign up for their informative newsletters. You'll also get to hear when the famous Blessing of the Harvest Festival is to be held (usually the second Saturday in February), a landmark event – barefoot crushing, label competitions, barbecued lobster and other good food matched with super wines and much merriment well into the morning. You won't forget it.

The restaurant, Bread & Wine, spreads out onto the courtyard. It is run and managed by the renowned Le Quartier Français. It offers good, casual fare with a Mediterranean flair. You are certainly 'in the vineyard', with views through the lemon groves to the mountains beyond. Enjoy a relaxing lunch on a Huguenot farm where you'll feel little has changed for centuries.

Paarl

Pearl: this is the name given to the massive bald dome of granite above the town of Paarl. It glimmers like a pearl, reflecting fragments of vivid hues. These formations are interesting not just for their unusual shape but also for their geological significance. They are the second-largest granite outcrops in the world, measuring 654 metres above sea level. They forced their mammoth granite heads into the landscape some 500–600 million years ago, approximately 100 millions years before the Table Mountain structure protruded into the scene. There is an exhilarating walk up one of the boulders if you wish to enjoy breathtaking views.

Under instruction from Jan van Riebeeck, an exploration party made their way north to survey the land beyond Cape Town and to record their findings. From his post at the Castle, Jan van Riebeeck had named the imposing horizon 'the mountains of Africa'. They were seemingly impenetrable. In the party's search for a pass, they found a fertile valley teaming with wildlife. There was a wide river flowing north, which they named the Berg, meaning mountain river. The valley seemed ideal for expansion. It was during the governorship of Simon van der Stel that Paarl was established. The Dutch colonists settled here in 1687, followed by the French Huguenots in 1688. Their cultures and languages merged as the social fabric of the Cape formed. The Afrikaans language was officially launched in Paarl with the publication of *Die Patriot* in 1875. It is for this reason that the Language Monument strikes an imposing spire on the slopes of Paarl Mountain.

Paarl became a refuelling stop for travellers making their way inland. With the discovery of diamonds and gold in the South African interior in the late 19th century, there came a regular flow of travellers through Paarl. It was thus that Paarl became a bustling service and manufacturing centre as well as an agricultural hub.

A significant development in the South African wine industry was the formation of the KWV, which is headquartered in Paarl. At the turn of the 20th century, the KWV was established to protect the wine farmers from the price pressures of negotiating individually in the highly competitive European market. The farmers formed the co-op to enable them to act collectively and, essentially, to create a protective price cartel. KWV grew into a producer of note, with quaffers and award-winners. KWV's powers were legislated, effectively positioning it as a non-governmental regulatory body. Over the years, its powers were widened substantially. While the functions of the KWV may have had a positive impact at times, it became inappropriate in the modern market. The wine industry

began a substantial process of deregulation around 1990. The fruits of this newly found freedom are manifest in the multitude of new wine farms, innovative vineyard management and creative winemaking.

The Main Street in Paarl is dotted with historic Cape Dutch and Victorian buildings. The delicate candy-lace of the Victorian homes mingles with the swirls of the stout settlers' homes. Many of these are still residences – a tribute to the country atmosphere that pervades this busy town. In fact, many who work in Paarl still go home for lunch. Oak trees line the Main Street and beautiful gardens abound.

BACKSBERG ESTATE

**Road connecting R44 and R45
between Klapmuts & Franschhoek
Tel: (021) 875-5141
e-mail: info@backsberg.co.za
www.backsberg.co.za**

**WINEMAKER: Hardy Laubser
OWNER: Michael Back**

**OPEN: 8:30–5 Mon to Fri;
    8:30–1 Sat & non-religious holidays
CLOSED: Christmas, New Year's Day,
    Good Friday**

**TOURS: Self tours
TASTINGS: Nominal charge
WINES OFFERED FOR TASTING:
    Sauvignon Blanc, Sémillon, Chenin
    Blanc, Chardonnay, Rhine Riesling,
    Cabernet Sauvignon, Merlot,
    Pinotage, Shiraz, Pinot Noir, Malbec,
    Red blends, Cap Classique**

**RESTAURANT: None
PICNICS: Bring your own and lounge on
    the lawns**

Antique farm implements and a long drive under acacia trees welcome you to this large, family estate. Situated on the slopes of the Simonsberg, it is a casual and inviting winery. Picnic tables under the willows provide a beautiful setting where you can bring your lunch or let the kids roam. A stroll through the flower and herb gardens is a reward for the senses. The multiplicity of textures, colours and aromas hints at the flavours and smells you'll discover in the wines. There are always lots of birds singing and often farming activity rumbling in the background.

The tasting centre is a whitewashed Georgian-style building. There is ample room to taste or to wander around. Several interesting and unusual items are to be discovered in the tasting centre. They provide a personal glimpse into the history of winemaking in South Africa over the past century. Dotted about the lawns in front are antique crushing machines and presses and other interesting memorabilia from the winemaking days of yore.

Backsberg offers a video self-tour which is brief and informative. For those curious about wine-farming history, there is a museum of sorts filled with antique farm tools gathered over the years. This is tucked behind the cellar storage facility, which you can wander through as well.

The Back family immigrated from Lithuania in the early part of the 20th century and set about their avant-garde style of farming. Visionary is often used to describe them. Backsberg was one of the first, and is still one of the few, estates to make pot-still brandy. They were amongst the first to plant noble varietals decades ago – and they stuck to this when everyone else was replanting with bulk white grapes. Although innovation and advancement are a way of life at Backsberg, the underlying philosophy remains constant: to produce superb quality wines that are readily drinkable and affordable.

The family has also been at the forefront of industry redevelopment, focusing on economic and social independence for farm labourers throughout the Paarl Valley. The Freedom Road label is the fruition of a labour-empowerment initiative at Backsberg that has real substance. It is a joint venture that provides true ownership for the workers.

GLEN CARLOU

Road connecting R44 and R45
between Klapmuts & Franschhoek
Tel: (021) 875-5528
e-mail: glencarl@mweb.co.za

WINEMAKER: David Finlayson
OWNER: WM Finlayson/Hess Holding

OPEN: 8:30–4:45 Mon to Fri; 9–12:30 Sat
CLOSED: 25 & 26 December,
    1 & 2 January

TOURS: By appointment
TASTINGS: Nominal charge
WINES OFFERED FOR TASTING: Chenin
    Blanc, Chardonnay, Cabernet
    Sauvignon, Merlot, Pinot Noir, Red
    blends, Port

SHOP: Souvenirs
RESTAURANT: None
PICNICS: Not accommodated

Rock and thatch: Glen Carlou is reminiscent of a Swiss chalet. And yet it is African. It works.

Glen Carlou is on the crest of a hill. As you approach, the large stone walls introducing the estate's entrance stand prominently in the landscape. They are crafted from smooth, river stones of similar size and shape – all collected on the farm. They look like hundreds of eggs packed together in neat, parallel rows. The entrance gives way to columns of cypress flanking the steep cobblestone drive leading up to the winery.

Inside, the setting is somewhat dark – a welcome reprieve from the glaring sun. The railway-sleeper tables and chairs create a restaurant-like atmosphere. The gleaming tanks in the winery sprout up to the tasting area. It seems you can almost touch them: in fact, you can. During the harvest season, this area is a hive of activity and a must to see.

The patio deck is everyone's favourite. The view over the Paarl Valley is expansive and the boulders of Paarl Rock peek out behind the Paarl Mountains. In the winter, the high Ceres Mountains are often capped with snow. Look the other way to glimpse the curved horizon: it's the sea. Your view then turns across to the mountains marking the boundary of the Swartland.

The tasting guides are warm and friendly, and are also conversant with the wines. They show a loyalty and enthusiasm: many of the summer helpers return for several years. While you taste the wines try some of their estate cheese as well.

As you enjoy the environment, notice the irony: calm, classical music in the background contrasting in a humorous way with the crowing of roosters from the coop next door: a reminder that the elegance of wine is crafted from the art of farming.

HOOPENBURG

R101
Tel: (021) 884-4221
e-mail: hoopen@new.co.za
www.hoopenburgwines.co.za

WINEMAKER: Ernst Gouws
OWNER: Ernst Gouws

OPEN: 8:30–5 Mon to Fri; 10–1 Sat
CLOSED: 25 & 26 December,
    1 & 2 January, Easter

TOURS: By appointment
TASTINGS: Nominal charge, refundable
    with purchase of 6 bottles or more
WINES OFFERED FOR TASTING:
    Sauvignon Blanc, Chardonnay, Merlot,
    Pinotage, Cabernet Sauvignon, Pinot
    Noir

RESTAURANT: None
PICNICS: Not accommodated

Spread over the plains between Paarl and Stellenbosch, Hoopenburg stands like a ranch in the Australian outback. Clean wooden lines with a deep, covered porch conjure up images of sleeping in a hammock on a warm summer day. Quiet, secluded and yet conscious of the vast expanse of land and southern sky. The sun beats steadily. It's a good place to sit down on the front porch and enjoy the cool breeze.

Lavender, lemons and a cycad around the corner. The tasting cottage offers a most pleasant way to encounter the award-winning wines from this relatively new estate. The attention to detail and the precision throughout are refreshingly crisp – somewhat like the lemons. This is evident even in the vineyards, which surround the house like a hand-quilted blanket. The gardens are finely manicured, adding to the feeling that this homestead was carefully carved out of the landscape.

Hoopenburg is a bit like an Andrew Wyeth painting. There is a dream-like quality: something distant, something simple and at the same time complex. The beauty is not bold and striking but somehow it haunts your memory.

Hoopenburg is a quiet winery run by the Gouws family. You're likely to meet one of the daughters in the tasting room. When Ernst Gouws is not in the fields, he is often in the tasting centre. Their friendly demeanour is instantly welcoming. When they do need extra hands in the tasting centre, they call upon the oenology students from the nearby viticulture college, Elsenburg. They want to ensure that if you wish to know something about a wine-related aspect, then you will have that opportunity with whomever you meet at Hoopenburg.

The tasting cottage is cool and attractive on the inside. There is a myriad of pigeon holes, which are home to bottles of wine rather than birds. The smooth beechwood is soothing and the Nordic styling appropriate. The picnic tables on the porch provide a quiet place to enjoy the wines with a group of friends.

Tucked into the Paarl Mountains, Rhebokskloof is set with ponds, playgrounds, restaurants and a cool tasting area. It's like a family get-together in the park. The gardens are sculpted around the banks of the dam with the Du Toit's Mountains looming in the distance. The vineyards cling to the steep mountainside. In the winter, the contrast in colour and texture between the gardens and the dormant vineyards is bold. The lush, rolling lawns bordered by shrubs and flowers of all sorts have been the site for many picturesque weddings.

The wine-tasting area is a long hall on the side of the cellar. Murals lavishly embellish the walls, creating the illusion of extra space. But importantly, they have created an atmosphere that is different and interesting. It's a bit like the old English pubs, Friar Tuck and all. They have certainly produced an 'enjoy the elixir and good company' mood. The tasting area also spills out onto the courtyard banked by the maturation cellar and a magnificent granite boulder typical of Paarl Rock. Rhebokskloof probably has the best collection of shop items around. Great mementoes, all of which fit easily into suitcases.

The restaurant is in the Cape Dutch house. They serve a buffet, which caters for most diets. Their traditional Cape dishes are pretty good examples and worth trying. But save room for the koeksisters!

Rhebokskloof offers horse riding through the vineyards and the mountains. Champagne breakfasts and sundowners are popular. They even have overnight rides for the more adventurous.

Windmeul Road
connecting R44 & R45
Tel: (021) 863-8386
e-mail: rhebok@iafrica.com

WINEMAKERS: Daniël Langenhoven &
    Danielé Foot
OWNER: Keith Jenkins

OPEN: 9–5 Mon to Fri; 9–5 Sat & Sun
CLOSED: None

TOURS: By appointment
TASTINGS: No charge for individuals
WINES OFFERED FOR TASTING:
    Chardonnay, Weisser Riesling,
    Cabernet Sauvignon, Merlot,
    Gamay Noir

SHOP: Souvenirs
RESTAURANT: Buffet and à la carte
PICNICS: Not accommodated

FESTIVALS & PROGRAMMES: Wine Valley
    Horse Trails 083 226 8735

Special: there's no other description. Veenwouden exploded onto the scene in the mid-1990s with world-class wines. Its reputation only grows. The effort to reach such heights has relied on focused, hard work.

The search started when the Van der Walt family envisaged the production of world-class red wines in South Africa. But not any world-class reds, mind you. The reds they wanted to create had to compare favourably with the best of Pomerol and St Emilion. It took three years of research to find the right place. Soil was tested from cherished areas in Pomerol. Samples were taken from potential farms in South Africa and compared. Time after time, the answer was 'not the same – not the right farm'. And then the find – a small parcel of land just north of Paarl came onto the market. Ah yes, the soils matched. Finally.

Veenwouden is a family affair and everyone is passionate about the singularly red wine estate. Every decision is formulated around the founding vision of a true St Emilion style in the Cape. Wines from Pomerol–St Emilion are tasted regularly to retain focus on the benchmark. From his base in Switzerland, the international opera tenor Deon van der Walt perpetually provides insights about the Bordeaux goal.

Winemaker Marcel van der Walt handles the vineyards with the care of one looking after a child, checking each bunch, trimming each leaf. Such care and attention pervade Veenwouden. Marcel tests each barrel every week to confirm the consistent development of the wine. In the initial fermentation stage, he constantly monitors the colour to obtain the maximum qualities. No more than five tons per hectare are yielded from the vineyards so as to maintain the highest quality.

The cellar was designed as a small auditorium, where Deon occasionally performs private recitals. The walls have been attractively hand-painted. All in all, quality is everywhere.

The name Veenwouden? It is a small village in Friesland in The Netherlands, from where the first Van der Walts immigrated in 1727.

An appointment is necessary to visit this unique winery, and you should book well in advance.

R45
Tel: (021) 872-6806

WINEMAKER: Marcel van der Walt
OWNER: Deon van der Walt

OPEN: By appointment only
CLOSED: Weekends and public holidays

TOURS: By appointment
TASTINGS: Moderate charge
WINES OFFERED FOR TASTING: Merlot,
**   Bordeaux blends, Malbec blend**

RESTAURANT: None
PICNICS: Not accommodated

VILLIERA ESTATE

R304
(Klapmuts–Stellenbosch)
Tel: (021) 882-2002/3
e-mail: villiera@mweb.co.za

WINEMAKERS: Jeff Grier & Anton Smal
OWNER: Grier Family

OPEN: 8:30–5 Mon to Fri, 8:30–1 Sat
CLOSED: Christmas, New Year's Day,
   Good Friday

TOURS: By appointment with guide.
   Self-tours are well organised
TASTINGS: No charge for individuals
WINES OFFERED FOR TASTING:
   Sauvignon Blanc, Sémillon, Chenin
   Blanc, Chardonnay, Rhine Riesling,
   Gewürztraminer, Merlot, Cabernet
   Sauvignon, Pinotage, Pinot Noir,
   Shiraz, Red blends, Cap Classique

RESTAURANT: None
PICNICS: Not accommodated

FESTIVALS & PROGRAMMES: St Vincent's
   Day Celebration, Toast to Art

Villiera is an agapanthus lover's delight. Fields and fields of the elegant chandelier umbels border the drive, providing a rich tapestry to lead you to the tasting centre.

Upon entering the tasting room, you may notice a cinnamon and apple scent, barely discernible and delicate like a perfume. In looking for the source, observe the finely carved beam in the centre of the room, with grapes, vines and leaves entwined. In the corner, the cast-iron chair appears to have belonged to the railway era with its beautiful scene of African antelope. Paintings in lively colours in the various alcoves seem to be by the same artist but haven't been signed. Yet like the scent and other curiosities, their origins do not matter so much as their pleasing effect.

The tasting centre is best described as convivial. It's like a big, warm farm-style kitchen, with U-shaped tasting alcoves and lots of homespun warmth and down-to-earth friendliness. It all reminds one of the small *osterias* tucked away in the hills of the Tuscan countryside. Instead of antipasto, you are served a vast selection of wines ranging from sweet to dry, white to red, and, of course, some bubbly. There is also a port you can sample. I overheard a customer ask the tasting guide what South Africans are going to call port when the agreement with the European Union banning the terms 'port' and 'sherry' comes into effect. She very quickly quipped 'ex-port'.

In the summer season, there is an outside patio area set in the shade of the oak trees. If you have an afternoon to relax with friends and want to do something out of the ordinary, try a game of boules. It is a popular social event among the winemakers, who periodically gather together for an afternoon of game and merriment.

One of the most remarkable features at Villiera is their self-tour. They encourage you to look around their operation. If they aren't busy, they're more than willing to provide a guided tour. For an estate that does not get busloads of people, the self-tour is well planned and clearly marked. You proceed on catwalks above the tanks and around the crushing area. In the harvest season, the place is bustling beneath you. The fermentation area also has a seating deck, where you can sit inside, or outside, and take in the view.

In the movie *French Kiss*, Kevin Kline's character passionately protects a fledgeling vine in his zany pursuit to buy a small parcel of family land in rural France. Meg Ryan portrays a candid Romantic awakened to her dreams of planting roots. Together they begin their quest to nurture the complex beauty of nature through the vines and the wines. In the closing scene, Ryan wanders through the French countryside around a simple country house.

This may seem an odd comparison to make with an estate at the foot of Africa. But as you turn off the country road to Welgemeend's gravel drive, you'll begin to understand. A simple home at the far reaches of the vineyards is your destination. There are vineyards on either side and just enough room for your car. With bush vines and trellised vines all around, it feels as though you're actually wandering in the vineyards – not on a road. And if you see Louise Hofmeyr in the fields, you'll instantly recognise the comparison.

Driving into Welgemeend has a completely different feel from any other winery. Every available corner is planted with vine. The buildings are simple and functional. There are no hints of opulence or fanfare anywhere. You'll probably be the only visitors. It's a rural village farm, where someone will come out of the house to greet you.

Welgemeend means 'good intentions'. The name was taken from the last working vineyard in the centre of Cape Town, which was owned by the Hofmeyrs' forebears. A school, houses and restaurants have replaced the city vineyards but reference to Welgemeend and the Hofmeyrs can be found in surrounding street names.

This family winery is the product of a passionate pursuit to coax the mysteries of nature into South Africa's first bordeaux blend. A husband–wife team, Billy and Ursula Hofmeyr founded Welgemeend in the early 1970s. The late Billy Hofmeyr blended his bordeaux-style wines in 1979 – a first for the country. Ursula is still the efficient farm manager and often the person who helps with the tastings.

As evidence of the Hofmeyrs' enthusiasm, rows and rows of countless bottles of wine sampled over the years line the countrified tasting-room. When Billy retired from winemaking, the chalice was handed to daughter Louise. Like her father, Louise has a natural talent with wine. Her sensitive style flows through to the wines. But always she has her eye on the bordeaux blend in its classic French style.

R101
Tel: (021) 875-5210
e-mail: welgemeend@worldonline.co.za

WINEMAKER: Louise Hofmeyr
OWNER: Hofmeyr Family

OPEN: 2–4 Wed, 9–12:30 Sat,
   other times by appointment
CLOSED: Christmas, New Year's Day,
   Good Friday

TOURS: None
TASTINGS: No charge for individuals
WINES OFFERED FOR TASTING: Red
   Bordeaux blends

RESTAURANT: None
PICNICS: Not accommodated

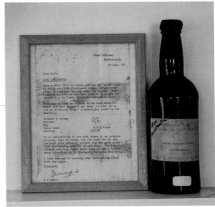

97

Durbanville

Please note that Durbanville is definitely not part of the Paarl wine region. It's just that I often head up the back way to Paarl through Durbanville. It's off the highway, on a remote country lane, making the journey to Paarl more exotic.

Nitida Cellars can be found in the hills of Durbanville, overlooking the valley to Stellenbosch and False Bay. Cool breezes waft up to this new, contemporary winery.

From the bustling commercial centre of Durbanville and sprawling residential communities, the road narrows. Suddenly, you are on a leafy country road surrounded by vineyards. It is a mind-warp, because all you did was blink and you're in a different world. A grove of oaks lines the road, creating a deeply shadowed tunnel. As you emerge, you're in a rural valley carpeted in verdant green.

Nitida Cellars is around a bend near the crest of a slope. The 'mountains of Africa' strike a distant pose on the horizon. The gravel road rambles around to the tasting centre, housed in the barrel-maturation cellar. The large, polished logs are notable features. Their rich colours and sensuous contours exude a homely warmth and yet, at the same time, stand individually as sculptural, contemporary pieces of art.

The estate is named after a type of protea that grows wild in the area and prolifically on the farm. As with most botanical names, *nitida* is of Latin origin, meaning bright, shiny, healthy, refined and cultured. These characteristics embodied the Vellers' vision and Nitida was, thus, the perfect name for their wines.

A family-owned and -operated winery, Nitida is the smallest winery in the Durbanville area. As Bernhard Veller will ebulliently tell you, producing just 5000 cases a year allows them the flexibility to experiment with innovations and to challenge their creativity. His contention is paying dividends. In a very short time, they have made an impressive name for Nitida wines.

M13, Durbanville
Tel: (021) 976-1467
e-mail: nitida@ct.lia.net

WINEMAKER: Bernhard Veller
OWNER: Veller Family

OPEN: 9–5 Mon to Fri, 9–1 Sat,
call in winter
CLOSED: Christmas, Good Friday

TOURS: Cellar tours by appointment
TASTINGS: No charge
WINES OFFERED FOR TASTING:
Sauvignon Blanc, Chardonnay,
Cabernet Sauvignon, Shiraz, Pinotage

RESTAURANT: None
PICNICS: Not accommodated

A Vineyard Year

September–November

Spring is the time for active new growth. Baby grapes are visible from about the end of October. New vineyards are watered to establish their root structure. The vineyards are lightly irrigated to prevent the roots from drying out later in the summer season. The soils are tilled and cleaned around the vines. Most vineyards are sprayed to prevent the onset of diseases and pests.

Red wines from previous vintages are generally released.

SPRING FESTIVALS
• Spier offers a wide range of evening events throughout spring and summer
• Hazendal has concert evenings and dinner events starting in October
• Stellenbosch Food & Wine Festival (October)

December–February

Summers are usually warm to hot, with occasional rain. In spring and early summer, there are strong prevailing winds from the Antarctic. The cool breezes and steady sunshine enhance the berry development without destroying the fruit.

The soil is left alone, except for weed control. Young vines are tied to trellises and vine leaves are trimmed to control sunlight. By January, the berries are clearly visible as bunches of grapes. Harvesting usually begins in February.

SUMMER FESTIVALS
• Villiera, St Vincent's Eve Festival (January)
• Môreson, Nouveau Festival (February)
• Don't forget about Spier and Hazendal

March–May

This is a very busy time in the vineyards. March is the tail end of the harvest season. The vineyards are irrigated, fertilised, tilled and prepared for new plantings. Preparations for winter pruning get under way.

In the winery, the grapes are fermented and then stored in tanks and barrels for maturation.

AUTUMN FESTIVALS
• Boschendal, Moonlight Pique-Niques (March)
• Paarl Nouveau Wine Festival (April)
• Nova Constantia, Art and textile exhibitions (May)
• Paarl Flower Show (May)

June–August

Winters are notable for cool sunny days with bouts of rain throughout. The vines are dormant. Abundant rains are important for deep saturation of the sub-strata, from where the vines absorb water during the growing season. The soil is tilled and fertilised. New vineyards are planted. Existing vines are pruned.

Unwooded white wines are released in June/July. Red wines are bottled from May through August and some vintages may be released.

WINTER FESTIVALS
• Boschendal, Bastille Day (July)
• Franschhoek Village, Bastille Day (July)
• Waterfront Wine Festival (end-August)
• Villiera, Toast to Art (throughout winter)

WHERE TO FIND WHAT

There are many restaurants and hotels throughout the Cape Peninsula and Winelands. As with the wineries, the list reflects my own views on and preferences for some of the restaurants in each area. Ask around or get a good food guide to find what suits you. With regard to the hotels, I've stayed in some but not all. My selection is based on references from trusted friends and family. I have not included hotels in Cape Town as there are too

CONSTANTIA

RESTAURANTS

Buitenverwachting (s)
Klein Constantia Road
794-3522
Sublime views and food in a demure atmosphere.

Uitsig (sc)
Constantia Uitsig
M2 on the Tokai Road
794-4480
Chic and tranquil with spellbinding views. The cuisine is Provençal touched by Tuscany with all the nuances in between.

La Colombe (sc)
Constantia Uitsig
M2 on the Tokai Road
794-2390
Snug and enchanting with tantalising modern French cuisine.

Spaanschemat River Café (c)
Constantia Uitsig
M2 on the Tokai Road
794-3010
Casual gourmet for lazy lunches.

Steenberg Restaurant (sc)
Steenberg Estate
Tokai and Steenberg Roads
713-2222
Cosy Cape Dutch in original wine cellar.

Melissa's: The Food Shop (c)
Constantia Village Courtyard
794-4696
Unassumingly obvious people-watching with granola and salads on the side.

ACCOMMODATION

Constantia Uitsig Country Hotel
794-4480
www.constantiauitsig.co.za

Steenberg Country Hotel
713-2222
www.steenberghotel.com

The Cellars-Hohenhort
794-2137
www.cellars-hohenhort.com

The Alphen
794-5011
www.alphen.co.za

The Andros
797-9777
andros@kingsley.co.za

Tulana
762-8500
tulana@global.co.za

The Sérénité Wellness Spa
713-1760
www.serenite.co.za

Kensington Place
424-4744
www.kensington-place.co.za

MUSEUMS

Groot Constantia Homestead
Groot Constantia Wine Museum

OTHER

Jill Blignaut Guided Walks
794-4836

STELLENBOSCH

RESTAURANTS

Governor's Hall (c-sc)
Lanzerac Manor & Winery
Lanzerac Road
886-5641
Whether inside or on the terrace, the ambience is great – food to match, from salads to 5-course meals.

The Green Door (c)
Delaire Winery
Helshoogte Pass R310
885-1756
Majestic views from the garden with fresh, Continental cuisine.

L'Auberge du Paysan (sc)
Firgrove Road
842-2008
French style in a cosy country house

96 Winery Road (c)
Winery Road off R44
842-2020
Good food. Warm, home-style setting with modern, colourful African art. Regular haunt of the wine set.

many. The information centres listed in the book can help you locate accommodation as well. My favourite reference guide is *Portfolio of Country Places*, which you can contact at (011) 880-3414 or at www.portfoliocollection.com.
All area codes are (021) unless noted.

KEY: (s)=smart, (sc)=smart casual, (c)=casual, (p)=picnic

Spier (c)
R310
809-1100
Several restaurants to choose from, including a picnic next to the river, or watch the kids chase ducks on the pond.

La Masseria (c)
Blaauwklippen Road
880-0266
For a truly Italian osteria in a cheesery. The owner even sings a cappella.

The Wijnhuis (c/sc)
corner Church & Andringa Streets
Stellenbosch
887-7196
For pasta, salad, fish or something more substantial. This is where the locals go.

ACCOMMODATION

d'Ouwe Werf
887-4608
www.ouwewerf.com

Lanzerac Manor and Winery
887-1132
www.lanzerac.co.za

Camberley Wines B&B
885-1176

Stonewall Wines B&B
855-3675

Eikendal Lodge B&B
855-3617
www.eikendal.com

L'Avenir Guest House
889-5001
lavenir@adept.co.za

Muratie Cottages
882-2330
muratie@kingsley.co.za

Rust en Vrede Guest House
855-4068
www.rustenvrede.com

MUSEUMS

Stellenryck Wine Museum
Oude Meester Brandy Museum
Oude Molen 'working' Brandy Museum
Blaauwklippen Vintners Museum

OTHER

Stellenbosch Historical Walks
883-9633 / 887-4931

Amoi Horse Trails
082-681-4285

Dan-Day Vineyard Horse Trails
082-485-5513

FRANSCHHOEK

RESTAURANTS

Bijoux (sc)
Huguenot Road
876-3474
Cozy fireplace in winter and garden terrace for summer. Continental.

Boschendal Le Pique-Nique (p)
Boschendal Estate
870-4274
Great, gourmet picnic baskets under the towering Cape pines. Reservations required.

Boschendal Restaurant (c/sc)
Boschendal
870-4274
An excellent selection of Cape cuisine.

Bread and Wine (c)
Môreson – Soleil du Matin
876-3692
Sister restaurant to Le Quartier Français. Dine overlooking lemon groves and mountains beyond. Wonderful Mediterranean dishes.

Frandeli (c)
Huguenot Road
876-3054
Great coffees, croissants and deli sandwiches.

Where to Find What

Franschhoek

Haute Cabrière (sc)
Lambrecht Road toward
Villiersdorp
876-3688
*In the maturation cellar, the venue is
sometimes controversial but all agree
the architecture is interesting and the
food outstanding.*

La Petite Ferme (c)
Franschhoek Pass on Villiersdorp
Road
876-3016
*Views from the terrace, and great
Franschhoek rainbow trout.*

Le Quartier Français (sc)
16 Huguenot Road
876-2151
*Relais & Châteaux. Fresh Provençal-
inspired cuisine in a calm garden setting.*

Monneaux (sc)
R45 just before village
876-3386
*Pleasant Continental food. Summer
in the garden, winter next to the fire.*

Topsi & Co (c)
7 Reservoir Street West
876-2952
*Eclectic. No regular menu. Dishes
depend on the ingredients at the
morning market. Sometimes unusual
but always excellent.*

ACCOMMODATION

Auberge Bligny B&B
876-3767
bligny@mweb.co.za

Auberge du Quartier Français
876-2151
www.lqf.co.za

Klein Oliphantshoek
876-2566
www.kleinoliphantshoek.com

Franschhoek Country House
876-3386
www.ecl.co.za

Grande Provence
876-2163
guesthouse@agustawines.com

La Couronne Hotel and Winery
876-2770
www.lacouronnehotel.co.za

La Petite Ferme Guest Suites
876-3016
lapetite@iafrica.com

MUSUEMS

Huguenot Monument
Huguenot Memorial Museum

OTHER

Mont Rochelle Equestrian Centre
083-300-4368

Paarl

RESTAURANTS

Bosman's (s)
Grande Roche Hotel
863-2727
*Relais Gourmands. Superb meals from
this 5-star Relais & Châteaux hotel.*

Rheboskloof Estate (c)
Windmeul Road
863-8386
*Converted homestead overlooking the
dam. Buffet and à la carte with something for everyone.*

ACCOMMODATION

Grande Roche Hotel
863-2727
www.granderoche.co.za

MUSEUMS

Language Monument
Paarl Museum

OTHER

Winelands Ballooning
863-3192
Wine Valley Horse Trails
083-226-8735
bikePOINT southafrica
083-430-8127

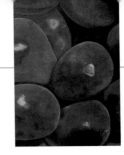

DIRECTORY OF CAPE WINERIES

This directory lists estates, wineries and co-operatives open to the public in Constantia, Durbanville, Franschhoek, Paarl and Stellenbosch, which includes the Helderberg area. The information was sourced from *John Platter's South African Wines 2000* with kind permission.

Agusta Wines Franschhoek 876-3195	Backsberg Paarl 875-5141	Blue Creek Stellenbosch 887-6938	Brenthurst Winery Paarl 863-1154	Coleraine Paarl 863-3443	De Zoete Inval Paarl 863-2375
Alto Estate Stellenbosch 881-3884	Barefoot Wine Co. Stellenbosch 887-9910	Bodega Paarl 988-2929	Buitenverwachting Constantia 794-5190	Cordoba Stellenbosch 855-3744	Diemersdal Durbanville 976-3361
Altydgedacht Durbanville 976-1295	Berg & Brook Paarl 874-2015	Boekenhoutskloof Franschhoek 876-3320	Cabrière Franschhoek 876-2630	Delaire Winery Stellenbosch 885-1756	Dieu Donné Franschhoek 876-2493
Amani Stellenbosch 905-1126	Bergkelder Stellenbosch 888-3400	Boland Wine Cellar Paarl 862-6190	Camberley Stellenbosch 885-1176	Delheim Stellenbosch 882-2033	Eaglevlei Paarl–Stellenbosch 880-1486
Ashanti Paarl 862-0789	Bernheim Winery Paarl 872-5618	Boschendal Franschhoek 870-4000	Cape Chamonix Franschhoek 876-2494	Dellrust Stellenbosch 842-2752	Eersterivier Cellar Stellenbosch 881-3886
Audacia Wines Stellenbosch 881-3052	Beyerskloof Stellenbosch 882-2135	Boschkloof Wines Stellenbosch 881-3293	Carisbrooke Stellenbosch 881-3034	De Trafford Wines Stellenbosch 880-1611	Eikehof Franschhoek 876-2469
Avondale Paarl 863-1976	Blaauwklippen Stellenbosch 880-0133	Bottelary Winery Stellenbosch 882-2204	Clos Malverne Stellenbosch 882-2022	De Villiers Wines Paarl 863-8480	Eikendal Stellenbosch 855-1422
Avontuur Stellenbosch 855-3450	Bloemendal Durbanville 976-2682	Bredell Wines Stellenbosch 842-2478	Constantia Uitsig Constantia 794-1810	Devon Hill Stellenbosch 882-2453	Fairview Paarl 863-2450

107

Fort Simon
Stellenbosch
906-0304

Franschhoek Vineyards
Franschhoek
876-2086

Glen Carlou
Paarl
875-5528

Goede Hoop
Stellenbosch
903-6286

Goedgeloof/Kanu
Stellenbosch
881-3808

Graceland Vineyards
Stellenbosch
881-3121

Grangehurst
Stellenbosch
855-3625

Groot Constantia
Constantia
794-5128

Hartenberg
Stellenbosch
882-2541

Hazendal
Stellenbosch
903-5035

Helderberg Winery
Stellenbosch
842-2371

Helderkruin Winery
Stellenbosch
881-3899

Hoopenburg
Paarl–Stellenbosch
884-4221

JC le Roux
Stellenbosch
882-2590

Jean Daneel
Stellenbosch
889-6404

Jordan Vineyards
Stellenbosch
881-3441

Kaapzicht
Stellenbosch
906-1620

Kanonkop
Stellenbosch
884-4656

Klawervlei
Stellenbosch
882-2746

Klein Constantia
Constantia
794-5188

Klein Gustrouw
Stellenbosch
887-4556

Klein Simonsvlei
Paarl
875-5419

Kleine Zalze
Stellenbosch
880-0717

Knorhoek Wines
Stellenbosch
882-2627

Koelenhof Winery
Stellenbosch
882-2020

KWV International
Paarl
807-3900

Laborie
Paarl
807-3390

La Couronne
Franschhoek
876-2764

Laibach Vineyards
Stellenbosch
884-4511

La Motte
Franschhoek
876-3119

Landskroon
Paarl
863-1039

Lanzerac Cellars
Stellenbosch
886-5641

La Petite Ferme
Franschhoek
876-3016

L'Avenir
Stellenbosch
889-5001

Le Bonheur
Stellenbosch
875-5478

L'Émigré Wines
Stellenbosch
881-3702

Le Riche Wines
Stellenbosch
887-0789

Lievland
Stellenbosch
875-5226

Longridge
Stellenbosch
855-2004

L'Ormarins
Franschhoek
874-1026

Louisenhof
Stellenbosch
882-2632

Louisvale
Stellenbosch
882-2422

Meerendal
Durbanville
975-1655

Meerlust
Stellenbosch
843-3587

Mellasat
Paarl
862-4525

Middelvlei
Stellenbosch
883-2565

Mont Destin
Paarl
875-5040

Mont Rochelle
Franschhoek
876-3000

Mooiplaas
Stellenbosch
903-6273

Môreson
Franschhoek
876-3112

Morgenhof
Stellenbosch
889-5510

Morgenster
Stellenbosch
852-1738

Mont Rozier
Somerset West
858-1130

Muratie
Stellenbosch
882-2330

Nederburg
Paarl
862-3104

Neetlingshof
Stellenbosch
883-8988

Neil Ellis Wines
Stellenbosch
887-0649

Nelson's Creek
Paarl
863-8453

Nitida Cellars
Durbanville
976-1467

Onderkloof Wines
Stellenbosch
858-1538

Overgaauw
Stellenbosch
881-3815

Perdeberg Co-op
Paarl
863-8244

Plaisir de Merle
Franschhoek
874-1071

Post House Vineyards
Stellenbosch
842-2409

R & de R–
Fredericksburg
Paarl
874-1648

Remhoogte Farm
Stellenbosch
889-5005

Rhebokskloof
Paarl
863-8386

Rickety Bridge
Franschhoek
876-2129

Rozendal Farm
Stellenbosch
883-8737

Ruitersvlei
Paarl
863-1517

Rustenberg
Stellenbosch
809-1200

Rust en Vrede
Stellenbosch
881-3881

Saxenburg
Stellenbosch
903-6113

Seidelberg
Paarl
863-3495

Signal Hill
Stellenbosch
880-0908

Simonsig
Stellenbosch
888-4900

Simonsvlei
Paarl
863-3040

Slaley Cellars
Stellenbosch
882-2123

Somerbosch
Stellenbosch
855-3615

Sonop Winery
Paarl
887-2409

Spier Cellars
Stellenbosch
881-3351

Steenberg
Constantia
713-2211

Stellenbosch Farmers
Winery
Stellenbosch
808-7911

Stonewall
Stellenbosch
855-3675

Stony Brook
Franschhoek
876-2182

Sylvanvale Vineyards
Stellenbosch
882-2012

TenFiftySix
Franschhoek
551-2284

Thelema
Stellenbosch
885-1924

Uiterwyk
Stellenbosch
881-3711

Uitkyk
Stellenbosch
884-4416

Uva Mira Vineyards
Stellenbosch
880-1682

Veenwouden
Paarl
872-6806

Verdun
Stellenbosch
886-5884

Vergelegen
Stellenbosch
847-1334

Vergenoegd
Stellenbosch
843-3248

Villiera
Paarl–Stellenbosch
882-2003

Vlottenburg Winery
Stellenbosch
881-3828

Von Ortloff
Franschhoek
876-3432

Vredenheim
Stellenbosch
881-3878

Vriesenhof
Stellenbosch
880-0284

Warwick
Stellenbosch
884-4410

Waterford
Stellenbosch
880-0496

Welgemeend
Paarl
875-5210

Welmoed Wines
Stellenbosch
881-3800

Windmeul Winery
Paarl
863-8043

Yonder Hill
Stellenbosch
855-1008

Zandwijk
Paarl
863-2368

Zevenwacht Estate
Stellenbosch
903-5123

OTHER RESOURCES

BOOKS

John Platter's South African Wine Guide
Get the latest edition. A handy and essential reference on wine estates and wine ratings. (Annual)

Wine Magazine's Pocket Guide to Wines and Cellars of South Africa
A concise guide to wines and prices. (Annual)

ON THE NEWSSTAND

For a look at current issues and what's happening in the fields and where the hot festivals are, try *Wine Magazine*. Stellenbosch, Franschhoek and Paarl each produce their own newspapers, free of charge, on the industry and events in their areas. Usually available at a local grocer.

TOURISM INFORMATION CENTRES

Constantia & Durbanville
None specifically.
Cape Town Tourism Office, ground floor, Pinnacle Building (corner of Castle and Burg Streets)
Tel: (021) 426-4260
Fax: (021) 426-4266
e-mail: info@cape-town.org
web: www.cape-town.org

Stellenbosch
Stellenbosch Tourism & Information Bureau
36 Market Street
Tel: (021) 883-9633
Fax: (021) 883-8017
e-mail: eikestad@iafrica.com
web: www.wcapetourism.co.za

Franschhoek
Franschhoek Vallée Tourisme Information Centre
Main Road
Tel: (021) 876-3603
Fax: (021) 866-2768
e-mail: franschhoek@wine.co.za
web: www.franschhoekwines.co.za

Paarl
Paarl Tourism
216 Main Street
Tel: (021) 872-3829 / 872-4842
Fax: (021) 872-9376
e-mail: paarlinfo@cis.co.za
web: www.paarlwine.co.za

Enabling Tour Guides
Flamingo Adventure Tours
Pam and Jeff Taylor specialise in enabling tours of the Cape. Satour-registered guides, they organise everything from the tours to accommodation for the disabled visitor. Their vehicles are specially equipped for wheelchairs. Tours for the visual- and hearing-impaired can be arranged with advance notice.
Tel/Fax: (021) 557-4496,
cell: 082 450-2031,
e-mail: flamtour@iafrica.com

Vineyard Ventures
Gillian Stolzman and Glen Christie specialise in wineland and winery tours, offering tailor-made experiences. They will arrange guides for the visual- and hearing-impaired with advance notice.
Tel: (021) 434-8888, Fax: (021) 434-9999,
e-mail: vinven@iafrica.com